HOTSPOTS
CÔTE D

Written by Anwer Bati
Original photography by Anwer Bati
Front cover photography by Giovanni Simeone/World Pictures
Series design based on an original concept by Studio 183 Limited

Produced by Cambridge Publishing Management Limited
Project Editor: Rosalind Munro
Layout: Trevor Double
Maps: PC Graphics

Published by Thomas Cook Publishing
A division of Thomas Cook Tour Operations Limited
Company Registration No. 1450464 England
PO Box 227, Unit 18, Coningsby Road
Peterborough PE3 8SB, United Kingdom
email: books@thomascook.com
www.thomascookpublishing.com
+ 44 (0) 1733 416477

ISBN: 978-1-84157-763-0

First edition © 2007 Thomas Cook Publishing
Text © 2007 Thomas Cook Publishing
Maps © 2007 Thomas Cook Publishing
Project Editor: Diane Ashmore
Production/DTP: Steven Collins

Printed and bound in Spain by GraphyCems

CONTENTS

WHAT'S IN YOUR GUIDEBOOK?

Independent authors Impartial up-to-date information from our travel experts who meticulously source local knowledge.

Experience Thomas Cook's 165 years in the travel industry and guidebook publishing enriches every word with expertise you can trust.

Travel know-how Contributions by thousands of staff around the globe, each one living and breathing travel.

Editors Travel-publishing professionals, pulling everything together to craft a perfect blend of words, pictures, maps and design.

You, the traveller We deliver a practical, no-nonsense approach to information, geared to how you really use it.

● *Villas and yachts in Cap-Ferrat*

INTRODUCTION
Getting to know the Côte d'Azur

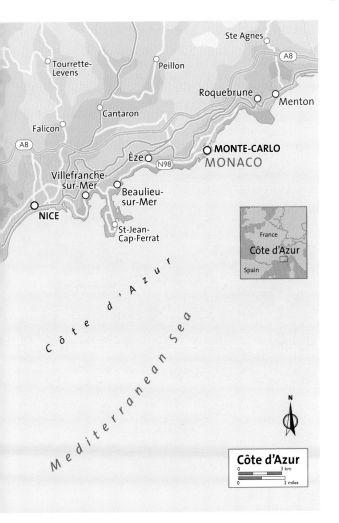

Getting to know the Côte d'Azur

The Côte d'Azur, the stretch of France's Mediterranean coast running to the Italian border, is about the most glamorous holiday destination in the world, as it has been since the 19th century. The area's resorts – Nice, Cannes, Antibes and Monte Carlo among them – remain glittering playgrounds for the rich and famous.

But despite the helicopters and private jets that buzz around the coast, and the gin palaces you'll see moored in the harbours, those on a budget can still have a fun time, particularly out of the high season, which runs from June to the end of August. Even so, nobody can pretend that it's a cheap place to visit.

⬤ *All sizes of yachts at Nice harbour*

The area is full of beaches, bars, hotels, restaurants, casinos and night clubs. And there is plenty of culture, too. Some of the world's greatest modern artists, including Picasso, Matisse and Chagall, lived locally. Many others visited in order to paint, inspired by the dazzling light of the coast. As a result, there are several fine local museums. So, whether you're interested in high life, high culture or both, you'll find something to interest you.

Difficult though it might be to imagine today, the coast, with its capes and harbours, once consisted of nothing much more than the city of Nice and a series of small towns and fishing villages. Then the British started visiting in the 19th century to get away from the winters back home, and it became a fashionable destination, with the fishing villages becoming major resorts boasting palace hotels. In the 1920s, the Americans also started to come, often in summer, in a wave immortalised by F Scott Fitzgerald in *Tender is the Night*. But the area only really became a major summer destination after World War II, with glitter added by the founding of the Cannes Film Festival and other events such as the Monaco Grand Prix. It also started to become heavily developed. Today the coast is mostly geared to tourists, the sailing fraternity and conferences and couldn't be more international. English is spoken widely.

Although you are likely to be visiting to be near the sea, the hills and hinterland behind the coastal strip offer a contrast to the bustle and buildings of the coast itself; the further inland you go the more peaceful it is. The hills are a popular destination throughout the year.

◓ *Tourist trains: an easy way to see a resort*

THE BEST OF THE CÔTE D'AZUR

The Côte d'Azur has something to offer pretty much anyone. There are beaches to laze on, bars and cafés to linger in, activities for the sporty, high-quality shopping, fine cuisine, history and culture.

TOP 10 ATTRACTIONS

- **Cannes Film Festival** Running for 12 days at the end of May, this is perhaps the defining event of the Côte d'Azur as it is today; glitzy, gaudy, frenetic and fun (see page 15).

- **A walk along La Croisette, Cannes** Stroll along the beautiful promenade to get a feel for the luxury of the Côte d'Azur. Then have lunch at one of the beach restaurants (see page 17).

- **Négresco Hotel and the promenade des Anglais, Nice** The Négresco is one of the most glamorous hotels in the world. And a walk along the seafront promenade will show you what attracted visitors to the city in the first place (see page 34).

- **Picasso Museum, Antibes** An impressive collection of the artist's work dating from when he used the museum building as his studio (see page 26).

- **Èze village** One of the most charming and spectacularly located hill villages in the whole of France, with stunning views of the coast (see page 46).

- **Villa Ephrussi de Rothschild, St-Jean-Cap-Ferrat** Amazing gardens, perched in one of the finest locations on the coast. The house itself boasts a varied collection of art and artefacts that only the seriously wealthy could ever acquire (see page 42).

- **Chagall Museum, Nice** One of the finest collections of works by one of the world's most popular modern artists, housed in a specially built museum (see page 36).

- **A drive along one of the Corniche roads** The spectacular views from these three winding coastal roads were shown to fine effect in Hitchcock's *To Catch A Thief* (see page 60).

- **Monte-Carlo Casino** It put Monte-Carlo on the map. It's worth at least seeing the grand exterior, even if you never wager a penny in its lavish interior (see page 50).

- **Chapelle du Rosaire (Matisse Chapel), Vence** This gem of a chapel was designed and decorated by Matisse. It is simple, peaceful and uplifting (see page 72).

○ *This castle in Antibes houses the Picasso Museum*

MUSEE D ANTIBES

MONUMENT HISTORIQUE

SYMBOLS KEY
The following symbols are used throughout this book:

ⓐ address   ① telephone   ⓕ fax   ⓔ email   ⓦ website address
🕒 opening times   Ⓝ public transport connections   ❶ important

---

The following symbols are used on the maps:

🅹 information office		⭕ city
✉ post office		⭕ large town
🛍 shopping		○ small town
✈ airport		◼ point of interest
➕ hospital		═ motorway
🛡 police station		― main road
🚌 bus station		⋯ minor road
🚆 railway station		― railway
✝ church		

❶ numbers denote featured cafés, restaurants & evening venues

---

RESTAURANT RATINGS
The following symbols after the name of each restaurant listed in this guide indicate the price of a typical three-course meal without drinks for one person. Remember that lunch or a set menu will often be cheaper.

£   under €20
££   between €20 and €60
£££   over €60

▶ *Cannes' elegant waterfront*

RESORTS
Places under the sun

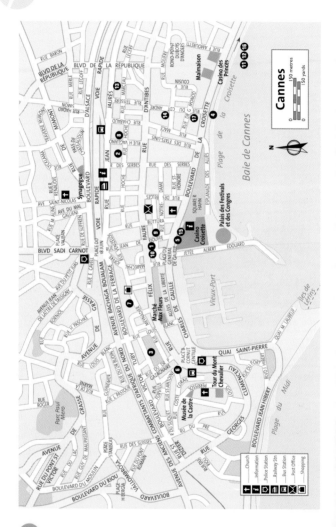

14

Cannes

Cannes, 25 km (15$^1/_2$ miles) west of Nice airport, is one of the most important tourist resorts in the world, and also about as glamorous as it gets. It buzzes most of the year, if not through regular tourism, then through a profusion of prestigious events (such as the famous Film Festival), conferences and trade fairs. As a result, prices are high (and even higher during the summer and major events), accommodation often needs to be booked far in advance, and traffic can be a nightmare.

Unlike Nice, Cannes has always lived and breathed tourism. It was little more than a fishing village until 1834, when Lord Brougham was forced to stop there on his way to Italy. He was so taken by the climate, the lovely setting and the sweep of its bay that he built a villa there. Other aristocrats and royalty followed his example. Soon a new port was built, and the first of the grand hotels for which Cannes is famous opened in 1858. As the resort developed, it divided into two distinct parts: the atmospheric Old Town and port to the west, with its bustling fish restaurants and the famous hill of Le Suquet; and modern Cannes to the east, with yacht marinas, casinos, the rather ugly Palais des Festivals conference centre and, of course, the promenade called La Croisette, lined with palace hotels looking onto miles of beach. Behind La Croisette are more shopping streets, smaller hotels and blocks of flats. Cannes changes more than any other resort on the coast; new hotels crop up, old ones seemingly past their prime get refurbished, last year's hot club or restaurant is out this year, and a new festival is added the next.

FILM FESTIVAL

The Cannes Film Festival first hit the headlines in 1946 and has been in the media spotlight ever since, not only for the tuxedoed international stars who attend its red-carpeted screenings at the Palais des Festivals or the wanabees who sashay down La Croisette, but also for the prestigious awards, such as the Palme d'Or, given by the festival's celebrity jury. Over the last couple of decades, the festival has also expanded to encompass a thriving film market. But it's not only the stars who descend on Cannes during those 12 days of May; they are joined by hordes of stargazers from around the world. You'll be lucky to glimpse a star, however, unless you gather round the Palais entrance before a screening, or hang around one of the grand hotels. For the most part, they get whisked off to glittering private parties on yachts and other luxurious locations.

And, although there are many film screenings you can attend at local cinemas, don't expect to be able to get into official shows; they're for the trade and journalists only.

BEACHES

Cannes has 7 km (4½ miles) of fine sandy beaches, almost all of which are open all year. At the west end of La Croisette is the public Plage du Casino. You have to pay at all the other 20-odd beaches, which line the main part of La Croisette with their colourful parasols. A number – the

⬥ La Croisette is a lovely place for a stroll

most fashionable – belong to the big hotels but can be used (for a fee) by non-residents. If you lunch in a hotel, you can swim free of charge but you have to pay for a sunlounger. A number of beaches offer windsurfing and waterskiing. For other public beaches you will have to go further west of La Croisette (La Bocca, for instance), or beyond to the east for beaches such as Mourre Rouge.

THINGS TO SEE & DO

Cannes has surprisingly few formal attractions. Most people are happy to while away the time in a beach restaurant or a Croisette café. A wander round the narrow streets of the Old Town and up Le Suquet is always an attractive option. And having lunch at one of the seafood restaurants in the old port area could almost make you think you were, after all, in a fishing village. Otherwise, walking along the elegant La Croisette (particularly in the morning and at sunset) is to take part in a favourite local activity. And popping into one of the palace hotels and having a drink in their bars or on their terraces might cost an arm and a leg but will certainly give you a taste for the high life. The domed Carlton, built in 1912, is the social hub of the Film Festival; the Majestic, originally built in 1863 but rebuilt in 1926, is almost as famous; and the Martinez, sitting like a stately liner at the eastern end of La Croisette, was built in 1929 in art deco style.

Then there's the shopping. There are ordinary shops in town, the covered Forville food market and rue Meynardier in the old town, but generally, think luxury. Cannes is so synonymous with designer shopping that it has, would you believe, its own Shopping Festival in January.

If you want a bit more adrenalin in your holiday, you can do all types of watersports here. The Tourist Information office and website have full details.

Tourist Information ⓐ Esplanade Georges Pompidou & rue Jean Jaurès (railway station) ⓘ 04 92 99 84 22 & 04 93 99 19 77 ⓦ www.cannes-on-line.com

Îles de Lérins

You can take a boat trip to the beautiful Îles de Lérins (Ste-Marguerite and St-Honarat), only 15 minutes from the old port with the company Planaria. St-Honarat has an ancient fortified monastery, from which you can get fine views of the coast. Ste-Marguerite is a good place to picnic. It has pine forests and a fort, in which the mysterious Man in the Iron Mask was imprisoned. The fort also houses the Musée de la Mer (Museum of the Sea), with artefacts found under water nearby.

St-Honorat Monastery ❶ 04 92 99 54 00 ❷ 10.30–12.30 & 14.30–17.00 July–mid-Sept; 09.00–17.00 mid-Sept–June ❶ Admission charge July–mid-Sept

Ste-Marguerite Fort ❶ 04 93 43 18 17 ❷ 10.30–17.45 Apr–Sept; 10.30–13.15 & 14.15–16.45 Tues–Sun, Oct–Mar ❶ Admission charge

Planaria ❷ Quay des Îles ❶ 04 92 98 71 38 ❷ Daily departures 09.00–17.30

Malmaison

This is a lovely 19th-century villa on La Croisette housing major temporary art exhibitions. For the latest news and information on what's on, visit the Tourist Information office.

❷ 47 La Croisette ❶ 04 97 06 44 90 ❷ 10.30–13.00 & 14.30–18.30 Tues–Sun, Apr–June; 11.00–20.00 Tues–Thur & Sat–Sun, 11.00–22.00 Fri, July–mid-Sept; 11.00–20.00 Tues–Sun, mid-Sept–Mar
❶ Admission charge

Musée de la Castre

This eclectic collection is housed in a refuge and watchtower built by monks in the 11th century on the hill of Le Suquet. It's full of antiquities including Egyptian mummies, archaeological objects, Chinese porcelain and other artefacts from Asia, the Pacific and ancient civilisations. Modern works of art are also on display. You can get great views from the tower.

❷ Place de la Castre ❶ 04 93 38 55 26 ❷ 10.00–13.00 & 15.00–19.00 Tues–Sun, June–Aug; closes 18.00 Apr, May & Sept; closes 17.00 Oct–Mar
❶ Admission charge

Restaurants & bars

Cannes has over 300 restaurants of all types, from top gastronomic experiences to pizzerias, as well as Vietnamese, Thai, Italian, Chinese, Moroccan and Indian restaurants. As a general rule, the further back you are from La Croisette, the cheaper your meal will be.

TAKING A BREAK

La Galette de Marie £ ❶ Crêpes and galettes. ⊚ 9 rue Bivouac Napoléon ❶ 04 93 68 15 13 ● Closed Sun Sept–June

Pause Café £ ❷ A decent café near the railway station. ⊚ 39 rue Hoche ❶ 04 93 39 83 03 ● Daytime only

La Taverne Lucullus £ ❸ Cheap, cheerful, good lunches in the old town. ⊚ 4 place de Marché Forville ❶ 04 93 39 32 74 ● Closed Mon

Cannes Beach ££ ❹ Complete with yellow parasols, this is one of the best choices on the beach. Reasonable prices for a drink or a range of simple food, from sandwiches and salads to more substantial dishes including good seafood. The restaurant (open from late morning until early evening) is run by the owners of the hip, competitively priced and conveniently located Cézanne and Renoir hotels. And if you stay there, packages include lunch and use of the beach. ⊚ Boulevard de la Croisette (opposite the Grand Hotel) ❶ 04 93 38 14 59 ● Closed mid-Nov–mid-Dec

La Maison du Porto ££ ❺ Just off La Croisette. Slowish service, but good pizza, pasta, ice creams and seafood. Or you can just get a drink. ⊚ 1 sq Mérimée ❶ 04 93 39 20 10 ● 08.00–24.00

AFTER DARK

Apart from Nice, nowhere else on the coast can match up to Cannes' throbbing, sophisticated and varied nightlife. From cocktail lounges to discos to late night piano bars and nightclubs. And there are no fewer than three casinos, more than in any other French town. If you want to go to a casino, you'll need to take your passport with you. And after you've let your hair down, a late stroll along La Croisette is just the thing to clear your head.

Restaurants

Auberge Provençal £–££ ❻ The oldest restaurant in Cannes, serving local specialities. ❸ 10 rue St-Antoine ❶ 04 92 99 27 17

Aux Bons Enfants £–££ ❼ Simple traditional Provençal food in a cosy atmosphere, and a favourite with locals. No credit cards, and no telephone bookings. ❸ 80 rue Meynadier ❷ Closed Sun & mid-Nov–early Jan

Bistrot Margaux £–££ ❽ Local food and wine in a traditional bistro. ❸ 14 rue Hélène Vagliano ❶ 04 93 38 68 68 ❷ Closed Sun

Café Roma £–££ ❾ Good pasta, grills and a terrace attract the trendy to this venue, which stays open late. ❸ 1 square Mérimée ❶ 04 93 38 05 04

Le Dauphin £–££ ❿ Pizzas and other dishes. The only restaurant in Cannes to be open around the clock. ❸ 1 rue Bivouac Napoléon ❶ 04 93 39 22 73

La Palme d'Or £££ ⓫ The best-known gastronomic restaurant in Cannes, famed for chef Christian Willer's superb creations in the luxurious Martinez hotel. ❸ 73 boulevard de la Croisette ❶ 04 92 98 74 14 ❷ Closed Sun, Mon (except during major conferences and festivals), Nov & Feb

Bars

L'Amiral ⓬ At the Martinez hotel, this popular piano bar is one of the most luxurious venues in town. ❸ 73 boulevard de la Croisette ❶ 04 92 98 73 00 ❷ 10.00–02.00

Le Bar à Vin ⓭   It serves a wide range of wines, as well as small snacks.
ⓐ 10 rue Marceau ❶ 04 93 38 45 48 ⓛ Evenings only

Le Chokko ⓮   Popular contemporary bar with a DJ. ⓐ 15 rue des Frères
Pradinac ❶ 06 18 09 70 28 ⓛ 18.00–02.00, closed Sun

La Farafalla ⓯   Good late night bar opposite the Palais des Festivals.
ⓐ 1 boulevard de la Croisette ❶ 04 93 68 93 00

Discos
Le Bâoli ⓰   Huge and luxurious, usually thronging, this is *the* disco in
Cannes, with a view of the bay. ⓐ Port Pierre Canto, boulevard de la
Croisette ❶ 04 93 43 03 43 ⓛ Closed Nov–Apr

Le Loft ⓱   Young, smart and modern, with House music.
ⓐ 13 rue Docteur Gérard Monod ❶ 06 20 79 46 81

▲ *This 11th-century watchtower dominates the Old Town*

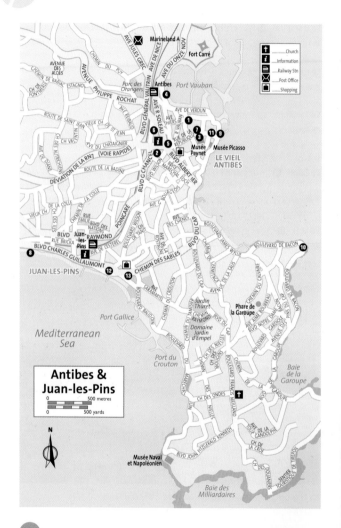

Antibes & Juan-les-Pins

Antibes was founded by the ancient Greeks as a trading post across the Baie des Anges from Nice. They called it Antipolis ('the city opposite'). It is still essentially a busy commercial city – the second biggest in the area after Nice – with substantial suburbs. But many visitors also go there, not least the yachting community who moor at the harbour, Port Vauban, the biggest marina in Europe. More casual, cheaper and less touristy than Cannes, it attracts people throughout the year. Antibes was fortified in the late 14th century, but it is only the 16th-century Fort Carré, near the harbour, and the sea fortifications that remain today. The place to go is the appealing Vieille Ville (Old Town) with its warren of small streets, and boutiques in rue James-Close. Graham Greene liked Antibes so much that he lived there for several years before his death.

The suburb of Juan-les-Pins, to the southeast of Antibes proper, with its pine forests (hence the name), is a major resort thanks to its sheltered location. It owes its development to the American millionaire Frank Jay Gould in the 1920s. It is very much a summer destination. Its lively, not to say brassy, atmosphere now attracts a young crowd, and nobody can claim that it is the byword for sophistication that it once was. It is now famous for its international jazz festival in July, founded in 1960, and the oldest in Europe.

A little further south of Antibes itself is the peaceful wooded peninsula of Cap d'Antibes, where the wealthy have their villas set in beautifully tended gardens. The cape is also home to the famous Hôtel du Cap Eden-Roc, perhaps the poshest hotel on the whole coast and featured in F Scott Fitzgerald's *Tender is the Night*. The roll call of celebrity guests since 1870, when it opened, is legendary. But the cape also has more modest hotels and restaurants for the rest of us to stay in, as well as superb views.

BEACHES

There are around 9.5 km (6 miles) of beaches in the area. The beach at Antibes itself starts off as gravel and then turns to sand, and is usually very crowded. You can also try the free, sandy Plage des Gravette. The sandy beaches of Juan-les-Pins are much more attractive. Many of the better ones are private and charge entry, but there are also free beaches. The beaches of Cap d'Antibes are also sandy. The Plage de la Garoupe and the Plage de la Salis are both public.

THINGS TO SEE & DO

There are events throughout the year. You can check with the Tourist Information website for full, up-to-date details.

Tourist Information Antibes ⓐ 11 place de Gaulle ⓣ 04 97 23 11 11
Tourist Information Juan-les-Pins ⓐ 51 boulevard Guillaumont ⓣ 04 97 23 11 10 ⓦ www.antibes-juanlespins.com

Fort Carré (Square Fortress)

First built in the 16th century and further fortified by the great military engineer Vauban in the 17th century, this was a French army base until 1996, when it was opened to the public. Guided tours only.

ⓐ Route du Bord de Mer, Antibes ⓣ 06 14 89 17 45 ⓛ 10.00–18.00 mid-June–mid-Sept; 10.00–16.30 mid-Sept–mid-June
❶ Admission charge

Jardin Thuret

A major botanical garden in Cap d'Antibes.

ⓐ Chemin Raymond, Antibes ⓣ 04 93 67 88 66 ⓛ 08.00–18.00 Mon–Fri, June–Oct; 08.30–17.30 Mon–Fri, Nov–May

Marineland

One of France's leading theme parks, centring on marine life but also offering other attractions such as a Wild West farm with ponies and a boat trip, a tropical bird sanctuary and three mini-golf courses. The highlights of the impressive main park are the dolphins, seals and sea lions, whales and sharks. No child will get bored here, and there's plenty to fascinate adults.

ⓐ 306 avenue Mozart, Antibes ❶ 04 93 33 49 49 ⓦ www.marineland.fr
🕐 10.00–22.30 June–Sept; 10.00–17.30 Sept–June; closed Jan
ⓘ Admission charge

Musée Naval et Napoléonien (Naval & Napoleonic Museum)
Artefacts associated with the great man and his landing at nearby
Golfe-Juan in 1815 after exile on Elba in this former military battery.
Great views, too.
ⓐ Batterie du Graillon, boulevard J-F Kennedy, Antibes ❶ 04 93 61 45 32
🕐 10.00–18.00 Tues–Sat, June–Sept; 10.00–16.30 Tues–Sat, Sept–June
ⓘ Admission charge

🔺 The 16th-century Fort Carré looks over Europe's largest marina

Musée Peynet et du Dessin Humoristique (Peynet & Cartoon Museum)

Celebrating the illustrator Raymond Peynet and other cartoonists.
🅐 Place Nationale, Antibes ☎ 04 92 90 54 30 🕐 10.00–12.00 &
14.00–18.00 Tues–Sun ⓘ Admission charge

Musée Picasso (Picasso Museum)

Housed in a 13th–16th-century castle, which Picasso was offered as a
studio in 1946. In gratitude, he donated a huge body of work to the
museum, making it one of the finest collections of his work in the world,
including ceramics as well as paintings he produced during the period
he worked here. There are also works by other major modern artists, such
as Ernst and Balthus, and regular temporary exhibitions. The museum
was closed for refurbishment until autumn 2007.
🅐 Château Grimaldi, place Mariéjol, Antibes ☎ 04 92 90 54 20
🕐 10.00–18.00 Tues–Sun, June–Sept; 10.00–12.00 & 14.00–18.00
Tues–Sun, Oct–May ⓘ Admission charge

Water sports

If you love water sports, then Antibes – where waterskiing was actually
born in the 1930s – is the place for you. You can also dive, windsurf or
hire a boat.
Diving Côté Plongée has children's ANMP and PADI courses. 🅐 Boulevard
Maréchal Juin, Antibes ☎ 06 72 74 34 94 🅦 www.coteplongee.com
Waterskiing École de Ski Nautique, Antibes 🅐 Plage Bretagne
☎ 06 13 61 51 17

MUSEUM PASS

Several of the museums have concessions for those under 18 or
over 65, and you can purchase a combined pass which covers a
number of museums. Get the pass and further details from any
Tourist Information office.

TAKING A BREAK

Adieu Bert'h £ ❶ A small, very good crêperie in the Old Town. ⓐ 26 rue Vauban, Antibes ❶ 04 93 34 78 84

Fleur de Sel £ ❷ A popular crêperie which also serves salads.
ⓐ 3 boulevard Foch, Antibes ❶ 04 93 34 58 25 ❶ 08.30–18.30, closed Sun

La Cascade £–££ ❸ A good, reasonable-value choice for lunch or dinner, serving steak, seafood, pizzas and pasta outdoors. ⓐ Place Nationale, Antibes ❶ 04 93 34 12 82 ❶ 12.00–13.00 & 19.00–23.00

Malouna £–££ ❹ Friendly bar and brasserie with a terrace serving pizza, pasta and more, near Port Vauban and popular with the yachting fraternity. ⓐ 9 avenue du 11 Novembre, Antibes ❶ 04 93 34 98 62 ❶ 07.30–24.00

Square Sud £–££ ❺ Plenty of choice and fast service in this brasserie. ⓐ 3 place Général de Gaulle, Antibes ❶ 04 93 34 86 30 ❶ 12.00–15.00 & 19.15–22.15, closed Sun

AFTER DARK

Restaurants
Le Galion £–££ ❻ Good meat and fish dishes in this traditional restaurant. ⓐ Avenue André Sella, Antibes ❶ 04 93 34 24 47 ❶ 12.00–14.30 & 19.00–23.30, closed Sun

L'Auberge Provençal ££ ❼ This old inn specialises in top-quality fish and seafood. You can sit inside or out in the large and pretty garden, or grab lunch at the seafood bar at the front. You can also buy seafood to take away. It has a number of pleasant rooms and is a convenient place to stay. ⓐ 61 place Nationale, Antibes ❶ 04 93 34 13 24

Bijou Plage ££ **8**   One of the prettiest and most chic restaurants in Juan-les-Pins, beachside. Serves fish and seafood. ⓐ Boulevard de Littoral, Juan-les-Pins ⓣ 04 93 61 39 07 ⓛ 12.00–14.15, 19.30–22.30

Les Vieux Murs ££ **9**   Built into the ramparts near the Picasso Museum, this place serves traditional Provençal food with a modern twist. Lighter food at lunch, and a fine view if you sit outside. ⓐ Promenade Amiral de Grasse, Antibes ⓣ 04 93 34 06 73 ⓛ 12.00–14.30 & 19.30–23.00, closed Mon lunch in summer, closed Mon in winter

Bacon £££ **10**   Antibes' most famous and stylish gastronomic restaurant. Try the *bouillabaisse* (fish stew). ⓐ Boulevard de Bacon, Antibes ⓣ 04 93 61 50 02 ⓛ 12.00–14.00 & 19.30–22.00, closed Mon, Tues lunch & Nov–Feb

La Jarre £££ **11**   A gastronomic restaurant with a courtyard serving Mediterranean cuisine. ⓐ 14 rue Saint Esprit, Antibes ⓣ 04 93 34 50 12 ⓛ 12.00–13.30 & 19.30–22.00, closed Wed

Bars
Although Antibes has numerous bars, there is much more nightlife in Juan-les-Pins. There are several lively places around the boulevards Baudoin and Président Wilson. Among those to try are:

Bar Fitzgerald **12**   At the Hotel Belles Rives. A sophisticated piano bar decorated in Jazz Age style. Smart casual dress code. ⓐ 33 boulevard Baudoin, Juan-les-Pins ⓣ 04 93 61 02 79 ⓛ From 15.00, closed Jan

Whisky à Gogo **13**   The most famous disco in Juan, if a little faded now. ⓐ 5 avenue Jacques Leonetti, Juan-les-Pins ⓣ 04 93 61 26 40 ⓛ 24.00–05.00, closed Sun–Thur off-season, closed mid-Jan–mid-Mar

⬤ *The beaches at Antibes are usually busy*

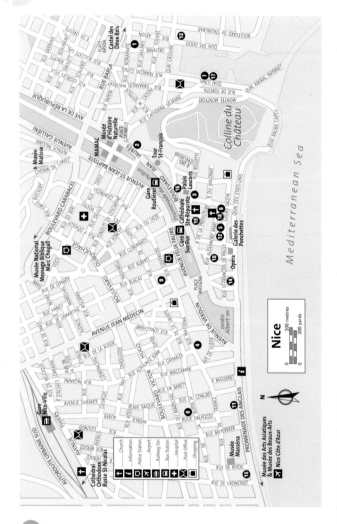

Nice

0   200 metres
0   200 yards

Church
Information
Police Station
Airport
Railway Stn
Bus Station
Hospital
Post Office
Shopping

Castel des Deux Rois

Musée d'Histoire Naturelle
MAMAC
Musée Matisse

Tour St-François

Cathédrale Ste-Réparate
Palais Lascaris

Gare Routière
Gare Felix Faure
SunBus

Galerie des Ponchettes

Opéra

Musée National Message Biblique Marc Chagall

Mediterranean Sea

Colline du Château

Jardin Albert 1er

Gare Nice-Ville

Cathédral Orthodoxe Russe St-Nicolas

Musée Masséna

Musée des Arts Asiatiques & Musée des Beaux-Arts
Nice Côte d'Azur

Nice

Nice is a major city as well as a resort. It's refined as well as hectic (and a little shady), with a large university and many expat residents adding to the mix. Built around the Baie des Anges, with hills rising behind it, it was founded by the ancient Greeks, who called it Nikêa. Later it was ruled by the Romans, who built on the hill of Cimiez; their amphitheatre is still there and is the site of some of the city's many events. The city then came under the rule of the counts of Provence. Eventually it was ruled by the Italian house of Savoy, and didn't become part of France until 1860. The Italian influence is still noticeable in the local lifestyle, food and the architecture of the Vieille Ville (the pre-18th-century Old Town) and its port.

The English started to winter in Nice in the late 18th century, and it was the English community, mainly aristocrats, who helped to develop it as a resort, not least by building the promenade des Anglais, which runs along the coast and is the southern border of the 'New' Town. The opening of a railway line in 1864 meant that tourism took off. Queen Victoria was among the distinguished visitors, as well as Russian aristocrats who built a cathedral in the city. The British influence is reflected in the names of some of the hotels on the palm-tree-lined promenade – West-End and Westminster for instance. But the grandest hotel of all is the Negresco, built in *belle époque* style in 1912. It is classified as a *monument historique* by the French government and, with its pink wedding cake dome, is Nice's most recognisable landmark.

Although parts of Nice are chic, others most certainly aren't, and the city long ago started to cater for ordinary visitors. You will find somewhere to eat or stay to suit your pocket year round, and there's plenty to do and see. Nice has good public transport, including trains which will take you along the coast from the Nice-Ville station. The bus service is excellent. A new tram system was being built at the time of writing, which will mean worse traffic during construction but improved service on completion.

BEACHES

There are several public beaches and 15 private beaches (for which you have to pay, but which have better facilities and choice of activities) along the 5 km (3 miles) of the Baie des Anges. All of them are pebble or shingle beaches. Most are off the promenade des Anglais, with some off the quai des États-Unis, its continuation. Activities include jet-skiing and parascending.

THINGS TO SEE & DO

If you're in Nice for just a short time, take a stroll along the promenade des Anglais and then head to the Old Town to enjoy its pastel-coloured buildings and maze of narrow streets. Everything is within walking distance. In the cours Saleya you will find the colourful flower and vegetable market, as well as bars and cafés. The port nearby is also worth visiting. Other attractions in the Old Town include:

Castel des Deux Rois (Two Kings Castle)
To the east of the port, off the avenue du Mont Alban, is this free, fun park which will appeal to young children. It has a giant chessboard, climbing frames, mini-golf and water sprays.

Colline du Château (Castle Hill)
There's no longer a castle, but the 92-m (300-ft) hill is a park. You can take a lift to the top (small charge) or walk up steps. Approach the hill from the eastern end of the quai des États-Unis. You will get great views from the top. The 19th-century Tour Bellanda, next to the hill, houses a naval museum.

Église de Ste-Rita
Also known as the Chapelle de l'Annonciation, this is a beautiful baroque church and much loved by the locals.
ⓐ 1 rue de la Poissonnerie ❶ 04 93 62 13 62 ❷ 07.30–12.00 & 14.30–18.30

Musée d'Histoire Naturelle (Natural History Museum)

There are all kinds of natural wonders and curiosities in Nice's oldest museum. And it's free.

ⓐ 60 boulevard Risso ⓣ 04 97 13 46 80 ⓦ www.mhnnice.com
ⓛ 10.00–18.00 Tues–Sun

🔺 *The cours Saleya has plenty of cafés as well as markets*

Palais Lascaris

This is a baroque palace with an impressive façade and staircase, and fine period furniture and tapestries. Built in the 17th century in the Genovese style.

ⓐ 15 rue Droite ❶ 04 93 62 05 54 ❷ 10.00–18.00 Tues–Sun

The New Town is also worth visiting. It has the Jardin de Albert 1er, a narrow band of greenery running back from the sea off the quai des États-Unis; a nice place to relax. And you shouldn't miss having a drink at the Hôtel Négresco and admiring its magnificent interior with a vast Aubusson carpet, a huge Baccarat chandelier and fine works of art. Other attractions include:

Cathédrale Orthodoxe Russe St-Nicolas

The Russian Cathedral is one of the most visited attractions in Nice. Inaugurated in 1912, it's famous for its gilded onion domes and an interior full of icons and frescoes.

● *You get a fine view of Nice from the Baie des Anges beach*

🅐 Boulevard du Tzaréwitch 📞 04 93 96 88 02 🕐 09.00–12.00 &
14.00–18.00 June–Sept; 14.30–17.30 Oct–May; closed for mass
10.00–12.00 Sun & on Orthodox holidays 🚌 Bus: 4, 7 ❶ Admission charge

Musée d'Art Moderne et d'Art Contemporain (MAMAC)

Opened in 1990 as part of an arts complex, the museum has striking
marble, steel and glass architecture, with four towers connected by
walkways. The collection of American and European art from the 1960s
onwards includes some big names, such as Warhol and Lichtenstein, as
well as local artists.

🅐 Promenade des Arts 📞 04 93 62 61 62 🅦 www.mamac-nice.org
🕐 10.00–18.00 Tues–Sun 🚌 Bus: 3, 5, 6, 16, 17 ❶ Admission charge except
first and third Sun of the month

Musée des Arts Asiatiques (Oriental Art Museum)

At the western end of the promenade des Anglais is a strikingly
contemporary minimalist building designed by Japanese architect Kenzo
Tange in 1998, with a splendid collection of Asian art and artefacts.
There is also a tea pavilion, where you can experience the Japanese tea
ceremony. The museum stands in the grounds of the 7-hectare (17-acre)
botanical garden, Parc Phoenix, which has the world's largest
greenhouse. It's worth visiting in its own right.

🅐 405 promenade des Anglais 📞 04 92 29 37 00 🅦 www.arts-
asiatiques.com 🕐 10.00–18.00 May–mid-Oct; 10.00–17.00 mid-Oct–Apr;
closed Tues 🚌 Bus: 9, 10, 23 to Arénas ❶ Admission charge except first
Sun of the month

Musée des Beaux-Arts (Fine Arts Museum)

An excellent collection ranging from the 17th century to the
Impressionists and early 20th-century artists, housed in a magnificent,
once-private villa built in 1876 for a Russian prince.

🅐 33 avenue des Baumettes 📞 04 92 15 28 28 🕐 10.00–18.00 Tues–Sun
🚌 Bus: 38 to Chéret ❶ Admission charge except first and third Sun of
the month

Musée Masséna

Housed in a splendid Empire building with an eclectic collection of porcelain, armour, the history of Nice and items connected to Napoleon and Nice's celebrated sons Marshal Masséna and Garibaldi. Closed for renovation until the end of 2007.
ⓐ 35 promenade des Anglais ⓣ 04 93 88 11 34

Further afield, to the north of the city, the hill of Cimiez has luxurious housing, Roman ruins and two important museums:

Musée Matisse

Henri Matisse lived and worked for much of his life in Nice until he died in 1954. This red 17th-century villa houses many of his paintings, as well as his book illustrations, engravings, sculptures and personal possessions. Closed for renovation until June 2007.
ⓐ 164 avenue des Arènes de Cimiez ⓣ 04 93 81 08 08
ⓦ www.musee-matisse-nice.org ⓛ 10.00–18.00 Wed–Mon
ⓝ Bus: 15, 17 to Arènes ⓘ Admission charge except first and third Sun of the month

Musée National Message Biblique Marc Chagall (Chagall Museum)

Built in 1972, this is a must if you're a fan of the Russian-born painter who lived on the Côte d'Azur. The collection centres on large canvases based on the Old Testament.
ⓐ Avenue de Ménard ⓣ 04 93 53 87 20 ⓦ www.musee-chagall.fr
ⓛ 10.00–18.00 Wed–Mon, July–Sept; 10.00–17.00 Wed–Mon, Oct–June
ⓝ Bus: 15 to Musée Chagall ⓘ Admission charge except first and third Sun of the month

TAKING A BREAK

Chez Pipo £ ❶ *Socca* (chickpea flour pancake) and other local specialities. ⓐ 13 rue Bavastro ⓣ 04 93 55 88 82 ⓛ Closed Mon

Chez René £ ❷   For *socca, pissaladière* (French pizza) and other snacks.
ⓐ 2 rue Miralheti ⓣ 04 93 92 05 73 ⓛ 09.00–23.00, closed Mon

Fennochio £ ❸   One of the best ice cream parlours in town.
ⓐ Place Rosetti ⓣ 04 93 80 72 52

La Pizza £ ❹   Excellent wood-fired pizzas in this popular mini-chain,
with two other branches in the same road. ⓐ 34 rue Masséna
ⓣ 04 93 87 70 29 ⓛ 11.00–01.00

⬤ *Built in 1912, Hôtel Negresco is now a historic monument*

L'Embarcadère £–££ ⑤   Seafood and pizzas are the speciality here; both are good. ⓐ 13 cours Saleya ⓣ 04 93 62 30 38

Au Long Cours ££ ⑥   This lively brasserie and pizzeria is favoured by locals as well as visitors. There is plenty of choice (including dishes of the day) and good service. Try the hearty *ravioli niçoise* or the equally generous *salade niçoise*. Most tables are outside. ⓐ 9 cours Saleya ⓣ 04 93 85 72 55

Bistrot du Port ££ ⑦   Excellent seafood and a fine view of the harbour. ⓐ 28 quai Lunel ⓣ 04 93 55 21 70 ⓛ 12.00–14.15 & 19.30–22.30, lunch only Tues, closed Wed

Hotel Windsor ££ ⑧   For a haven of peace, the garden or bar of this hotel is the place to go. The hotel itself is one of the most stylish in Nice, with rooms designed by local artists. Not far from the promenade des Anglais. ⓐ 11 rue Dalpozzo ⓣ 04 93 88 59 35

AFTER DARK

Restaurants
Brasserie Flo ££ ⑨   High-quality brasserie food (including seafood) in a converted old theatre. ⓐ 2–4 rue Sacha Guitry ⓣ 04 93 13 39 38 ⓛ 12.00–14.30, 19.00–24.00

L'Estoficada ££ ⑩   A simple but notable bistro serving local specialities. ⓐ 2 rue de l'Hôtel de Ville ⓣ 04 93 80 21 64

Queenie ££ ⑪   A convenient location and classic brasserie dishes, as well as *bouillabaisse* (fish stew). Live music on weekend evenings and a wide-screen TV showing sport. ⓐ 19 promenade des Anglais ⓣ 04 93 88 52 50

La Safari ££ ⑫   With a terrace on the cours Saleya, one of the best restaurants serving Niçoise cuisine in the area. ⓐ 1 cours Saleya ⓣ 04 93 80 14 44

L'Ane Rouge ££–£££ 🔞   One of Nice's best restaurants, in the old port, serving seafood and regional cuisine. ⓐ 7 quai Emmanuel ⓣ 04 93 89 49 63 ⓛ 12.00–14.00 & 19.00–22.00, closed Wed, Thur lunch

La Petite Maison ££–£££ 🔞   You'll get a warm welcome in this fashionable restaurant serving fine Provençal food. Very popular with locals. ⓐ 11 rue St-François de Paule ⓣ 04 93 92 59 59 ⓛ closed Sun

Le Chantecler £££ 🔞   The famous and luxurious restaurant of the Negresco has been blessed with many fine chefs over the years (currently Bruno Turbot), and gastronomic standards remain impeccably high. The hotel also has a much cheaper and more casual restaurant, La Rotonde, serving light dishes in cheerful surroundings. ⓐ 37 promenade des Anglais ⓣ 04 93 16 64 00

Bars
De Klomp 🔞   A Dutch-style pub. ⓐ 8 rue Mascoïnat ⓣ 04 93 92 42 85 ⓛ 17.30–02.30, closed Sun

Dizzy Club 🔞   A piano bar with a dance floor, live bands and a DJ. ⓐ 26 quai Lunel ⓣ 04 93 26 54 79 ⓛ 20.00–02.30

Ghost House 🔞   Small disco and bar, with a buzzy atmosphere. ⓐ 3 rue Barillerie ⓣ 04 93 92 93 33 ⓛ 19.30–02.30

Wayne's 🔞   Live music, theme nights and karaoke in this British-owned spot. ⓐ 15 rue de la Préfecture ⓣ 04 93 13 46 99 ⓛ 12.00–01.30

Villefranche-sur-Mer

Founded in the 14th century, Villefranche, 6 km (4 miles) east of Nice, is a pretty and lively town located in a beautiful sheltered bay. It is still a fishing port, but the depth of the water in the bay means that it is also often visited by naval vessels and cruise ships. The attractive harbour, with tall, pastel-coloured buildings, is lined with cafés and brasseries. Behind is the Old Town, running uphill, with stairs and narrow alleyways, including the vaulted rue Obscure. Although it doesn't have any great attractions or, indeed, any particularly special restaurants or hotels, it is one of the best choices on the coast for families or those on a budget. And as it is so near Nice, Beaulieu and other major resorts, it is a good base to set out from. There are several small shops selling souvenirs and local products.

BEACHES

Villefranche has a good, safe and sandy beach.

THINGS TO SEE & DO

Chapelle de St-Pierre des Pêcheurs

This 14th-century harbour chapel, once a sanctuary for local fishermen, is Villefranche's only really serious attraction. It has a painted exterior and, more notably, an interior with fresco murals by Jean Cocteau, created in 1956 when the artist lived in the town.

ⓐ Quai Courbet ❶ 04 93 76 90 70 ⏰ 10.00–12.00 & 15.00–19.00 Tues–Sun, June–Sept; 10.00–12.00 & 15.00–17.00 Tues–Sun, Oct–May ❶ Admission charge

Citadelle St-Elme

This impressive 16th-century fort, restored in 1981, houses the town hall, and contains some minor collections including the Goetz-Boumeester Museum, with around 100 pictures including works by Picasso and Miró, and an underwater archaeology museum. The chapel houses temporary art exhibitions. The building also has an auditorium and stages outdoor cinema and theatre shows in summer.

ⓐ Avenue Carnot ⓣ 04 93 76 33 27 ⓛ 09.00–12.00 & 14.30–19.00 Mon & Wed–Sat, July & Aug; 09.00–12.00 & 14.30–18.00 Mon & Wed–Sat, June & Sept; 09.00–12.00 & 14.00–17.30 Mon & Wed–Sat, Oct–May; closed Nov

TAKING A BREAK

Le Cosmo £–££ Just behind the harbour (but with a view from the terrace), this smart bar and brasserie is a popular venue for food or drinks. ⓐ 11 place Amélie Pollonais ⓣ 04 93 01 84 05 ⓛ 07.00–02.30

Beluga ££ Tapas and other fare in this restaurant and bar by the sea. ⓐ 3 quai Ponchardier ⓣ 04 93 80 28 34

La Mère Germaine ££ Right on the seafront. The best-known restaurant in Villefranche, serving good fish and meat, and Asian-inspired dishes (the owner lived in Tahiti). ⓐ Quai Courbet ⓣ 04 93 01 71 39 ⓛ 12.00–14.30 & 19.00–22.00

L'Oursin Bleu ££ Creative seafood cuisine. ⓐ 11 quai Amiral Courbet ⓣ 04 93 01 90 12 ⓛ Closed Tues

○ The tranquil bay of Villefranche

Beaulieu-sur-Mer & St-Jean-Cap-Ferrat

Beaulieu is a small, old and stately resort, somewhat faded after its former grandeur, but with a couple of grand hotels and some majestic villas. Its sheltered location makes it one of the warmest places on the coast, particularly in winter. It also has a yacht marina and a 19th-century casino, but nobody can claim that it's an animated place – except in the restaurants of the marina – or that much happens, especially at night.

The neighbouring resort of St-Jean-Cap-Ferrat must be one of the most expensive pieces of land in the world, full of millionaires' villas crowding the beautiful peninsula with its palm and pine trees, coves and headlands. Past inhabitants included David Niven, King Leopold II of Belgium and Somerset Maugham. It has a small harbour (St-Jean itself) with lively bars and restaurants, and several luxury hotels, although there are also some more modest family hotels. There's a pleasant walk along the coast from St-Jean to Beaulieu, ending at the western end of the Baie des Fourmis. A dramatic coastal footpath leads from Paloma beach to Pointe St-Hospice. There is also a lighthouse with fine views at the southern tip of the cape.

BEACHES

Beaulieu has two inviting, but stony, beaches: the Baie des Fourmis and the Petite Afrique. The three public beaches of Cap-Ferrat are rock and gravel, but pleasant nonetheless.

THINGS TO SEE & DO

Villa Ephrussi de Rothschild
One of the most stunningly situated villas on the whole coast, with an amazing series of gardens in different styles, and wonderful views. The palatial pink Italianate house itself has a diverse collection of art, furniture, tapestries and objects. There is also a café.
🅐 1 avenue Ephrussi de Rothschild, St-Jean-Cap-Ferrat ☎ 04 93 01 33 09

ⓦ www.villa-ephrussi.com ⓒ 10.00–18.00 Feb–June & Sept–Oct; 10.00–19.00 July & Aug; 14.00–18.00 Mon–Fri, 10.00–18.00 Sat & Sun, Nov–Jan ⓘ Admission charge

Villa Kérylos

Another millionaire's fantasy, this time that of archaeologist Theodore Reinach, who built this house in the early 1900s as a faithful reproduction of an ancient Greek villa. Sitting on a headland by the Baie des Fourmis and boasting excellent views, it's a very popular attraction but is confusingly signposted.

○ Villa Kérylos, one of the many spectacular villas in this area

📍 Impasse Gustave Eiffel, Beaulieu ☎ 04 93 01 01 44 🌐 www.villa-kerylos.com 🕐 10.00–18.00 Feb–June & Sept–Oct; 10.00–19.00 July & Aug; 14.00–18.00 Mon–Fri, 10.00–18.00 Sat & Sun, Nov–Jan ❶ Admission charge

Villa Tickets

You can buy a joint ticket that covers entrance for both the Villa Ephrussi de Rothschild and the Villa Kérylos.

Zoo-Parc Cap-Ferrat

Around 300 animals are in this small, well-planned zoo. Free parking.
📍 117 boulevard de Général de Gaulle, St-Jean-Cap-Ferrat ☎ 04 93 76 07 60 🌐 www.zoocapferrat.com 🕐 09.30–19.00 Apr–Oct; 09.30–17.30 Nov–Mar ❶ Admission charge

TAKING A BREAK

African Queen ££ In Beaulieu's yachting harbour, this is the most popular restaurant locally. Brasserie food and pizzas. 📍 Port de Plaisance, Beaulieu ☎ 04 93 01 10 85

Capitaine Cook ££ Fine fish served on a terrace. 📍 11 avenue Jean Mermoz, St-Jean-Cap-Ferrat ☎ 04 93 76 02 66 🕐 Closed Wed, & Thur lunch

Le Max ££ Good seafood in Beaulieu harbour. 📍 Port de Plaisance, Beaulieu ☎ 04 93 01 65 75 🕐 Closed Mon

Royal Riviera ££–£££ A formal restaurant with a more casual option by the pool for lunch, in a recently restored grand hotel. 📍 3 avenue Jean Monnet, St-Jean-Cap-Ferrat ☎ 04 93 76 31 00 🕐 Closed Dec–Feb

La Reserve de Beaulieu £££ One of the smartest hotels on the coast, with fine food, views and prices to match. Or just go for a drink. 📍 5 boulevard Général Leclerc, Beaulieu ☎ 04 93 01 00 01

⬥ *A corner of the lovely gardens at Villa Ephrussi de Rothschild*

RESORTS

Èze

Èze is the best-known hill village on the Côte d'Azur, and one of the most visited. It is beautifully restored, has a spectacular setting 429 m (1,400 ft) above the sea, and offers fabulous views of the coast. You can reach it from the coast via the Moyenne Corniche, the 'middle' level Corniche road. It has no real life other than tourism and is full of souvenir shops, art galleries and small, high-quality craft shops. You can park near the village entrance, then walk uphill through narrow alleys.

THINGS TO SEE & DO

Chapelle des Pénitents Blancs (Chapel of the White Penitents)
Built in the early 14th century, this is the oldest building in Èze.
🅐 Place du Planet

Usine Fragonard (Fragonard Pefume Factory)
Enjoy a free guided tour of this famous factory, going since 1926. There's also a shop.

🔺 The view over Èze – paradise

Moyenne Corniche, just outside the village ☎ 04 93 41 05 05
🌐 www.fragonard.com ⏰ 08.30–18.30 Feb–Oct; 08.30–12.00 &
14.00–18.30 Nov–Jan

Jardin Exotique (Exotic Garden)

On the site of the old castle and full of cacti and other desert plants, this
exotic garden offers great views of the coast.
📍 Rue du Château ☎ 04 93 41 10 30 ⏰ 09.00–20.00 July & Aug;
09.00–18.00 Sept–June ❶ Admission charge

TAKING A BREAK

Chez Clairette £ Snacks to take away or eat outside. 📍 Place du Général
de Gaulle ☎ 04 93 41 07 19 ⏰ Closed Nov–Feb

Auberge du Cheval Blanc £–££ Pizzas, as well as more elaborate food; outside tables. 📍 Place de la Colette ☎ 04 93 41 03 17 ⏰ Closed Wed & in Dec

Le Nid d'Aigle £–££ Open for breakfast and snacks as well as traditional
dishes 📍 1 rue du Château ☎ 04 93 41 19 08 ⏰ Closed Jan

Auberge de Troubadour ££ Honest Provençal food in a rustic setting.
📍 4 rue du Brec ☎ 04 93 41 19 03 ⏰ Closed Sun & Mon, mid-Nov–mid-Dec

Château Eza ££–£££ Haute cuisine with a reasonably priced lunch menu
at this luxury hotel. Tapas and other light food in the afternoon, after
lunch. 📍 Rue de la Pise ☎ 04 93 41 12 24 🌐 www.chateaueza.com
⏰ 12.00–15.00 (lunch) & 19.30–22.00 (dinner)

Château de la Chèvre d'Or £££ One of the most famous hotels on the
coast, with a star-studded guest list, and gastronomic food to match.
You can have lunch on the terrace with superb views. Otherwise just
go there for a drink and the view before or after lunch. 📍 Rue du Barri
☎ 04 92 10 66 66 🌐 www.chevredor.com ⏰ Closed Nov–early Mar

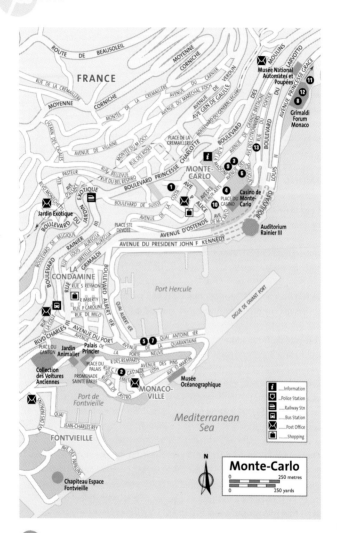

Musée National
Automates et
Poupées

Grimaldi
Forum
Monaco

FRANCE

MONTE
CARLO

Casino de
Monte-
Carlo

Jardin Exotique

Auditorium
Rainier III

LA
CONDAMINE

Port Hercule

Jardin
Animalier

Palais
Princier

Collection
des Voitures
Anciennes

MONACO-
VILLE

Musée
Océanographique

Port de
Fontvieille

Mediterranean
Sea

FONTVIEILLE

Chapiteau Espace
Fontvieille

i .....Information
.....Police Station
.....Railway Stn
.....Bus Station
.....Post Office
.....Shopping

N

Monte-Carlo

0   250 metres
0   250 yards

48

Monaco & Monte-Carlo

Somerset Maugham described this principality the size of Hyde Park as 'a sunny place for shady people', and despite the money and glamour, in many ways it still is. Monaco is the name not only of the principality, but also of the area around the royal palace. Monte-Carlo, with its high-rise buildings, is the area to the north of the port of Monaco.

It has been ruled by the Grimaldi family, who were also lords of much of the surrounding area, from 1308. The current sovereign is Prince Albert, son of the film star Grace Kelly who greatly added to the prestige of the place. Monaco has managed to hold on to its independence from France, even though the area around it became French in 1860. However, the loss of towns like Roquebrune and Menton meant that Charles III, the ruler at the time, had to find new sources of revenue, so he opened the famous casino in 1865. It was built on a rock called Monte-Carlo in his honour, and the principality became a wealthy resort as aristocratic tourists flocked there.

But it was the development of the resort from the 1950s onwards (by Albert's father Prince Rainier III, who died in 2005) that ensured that it would remain prosperous. The relaxed tax regime attracted super-rich expats from around the world. Land reclamation in the Fontvieille area (to the west), and the building of a new port and heliport there, also helped.

Today, Monaco is studded with luxury hotels and restaurants, and designer shops, and Monte-Carlo harbour is full of the mega yachts of the seriously rich. With so much money around, there is much pampering at steep prices. And wealthy visitors feel very safe in the midst of elaborate CCTV systems and a strong police presence. It's a year-round resort with a large number of attractions, and major events in most months, so hotels are generally pretty full and become packed to the rafters during major events like the Grand Prix. And then there's the nightlife. Although you may be able to see a lot on a day trip, you need deep pockets to enjoy the area fully. That said, you can walk to most places; there's a lot of uphill walking, but you'll find that the public lifts, with their marbled entrances, are pleasant and very useful.

BEACHES

There is only one major beach in the principality itself; the Plage de Lavorotto, which is public. The Monte-Carlo beach is technically in France. Both are off avenue Princesse Grace.

THINGS TO SEE & DO

A walk around the Old Town (Vieille Ville) near the palace, through the brightly coloured houses and narrow streets, is a pleasant way of getting an idea of what Monaco was like before all the high rises were built. For up-to-date information on events and sporting activities, check with the Tourist Information office.

Casino de Monte-Carlo

Designed by Charles Garnier (who also built the Paris Opera House), the most famous casino in the world is on most first-time visitors' must-see lists. From the outside, admire its grandeur and that of the square it's set in, and then have a look at the ornate interior. You can also pop in to the small but equally opulent opera house in the same building. It's free to visit the public areas, but not the gaming rooms. You should have your passport with you. If you want to gamble, men must wear a jacket and tie.
ⓐ Place du Casino ⓣ 92 16 20 00 ⓦ www.casino-monte-carlo.com
ⓛ 12.00 onwards

Collection des Voitures Anciennes (Classic Car Collection)

Prince Rainier's collection has around 100 cars dating from the beginning of the 20th century, all in immaculate condition.
ⓐ Terrasses de Fontvieille ⓣ 92 05 28 56 ⓦ www.palais.mc ⓛ 10.00–18.00
ⓘ Admission charge

Jardin Animalier (Zoo)

The small zoo has 250 animals collected by the late Prince Rainier. It overlooks the port of Fontvieille.

ⓐ Terrasses de Fontvieille ❶ 93 50 40 30 ⓦ www.palais.mc
🕘 09.00–12.00 & 14.00–19.00 June–Sept; 10.00–12.00 & 14.00–18.00
Mar–May; 10.00–12.00 & 14.00–17.00 Oct–Feb ❶ Admission charge

Jardin Exotique (Exotic Garden)

This surprisingly popular attraction was created on a rock face in 1933
and is full of cacti and other succulent plants accustomed to arid climes.
There is a cave (Grotte de l'Observatoire), once a Neolithic dwelling, with

▲ Monte-Carlo's skyscrapers surround the harbour

dramatic stalagmites and stalactites. And a Prehistoric Anthropology Museum exhibits the history of Stone Age man.

ⓐ 62 boulevard du Jardin Exotique ⓣ 93 15 29 80 ⓛ 09.00–19.00 mid-May–mid-Sept; 09.00–18.00/nightfall mid-Sept–mid-May ⓘ Admission charge

Musée National Automates et Poupées (National Museum of Automata & Dolls)

This very unusual and, you may find, fascinating museum, in a small pink villa designed by Charles Garnier, has one of the world's best collections of dolls, automata and mechanical toys from the 19th century.

ⓐ 17 avenue Princesse Grace ⓣ 93 30 91 26 ⓛ 10.00–18.30 Easter–Sept; 10.00–12.15 & 14.30–18.30 Oct–Easter ⓘ Admission charge

Musée Océanographique (Oceanographic Museum & Aquarium)

Founded in 1910, this is one of the best museums of its kind and few visitors leave unimpressed. The location is also grand. You will find an amazing variety of fish and other sea creatures in the aquarium. There are also displays of undersea objects and specimens. The terrace café on the top floor has fine views.

ⓐ Avenue Saint-Martin ⓣ 93 15 36 00 ⓦ www.oceano.mc ⓛ 09.30–19.00 Apr–June & Sept; 09.30–19.30 July & Aug; 10.00–18.00 Oct–Mar ⓘ Admission charge

Palais Princier (Prince's Palace)

The palace is closed when the prince is in residence (you'll see his red and white flag fluttering), but you can still catch the changing of the guard in the square in front of the palace at 11.55 every morning. The palace was originally built in the 13th century but has been extensively altered since, particularly in the 19th century. The highlights of the guided tour are the courtyard and the throne room, which contains several fine paintings. If you can't get into the palace, you can visit the separate Musée Napoléon in one of the wings. It contains relics associated with the emperor, and a section on Monaco's history.

Place du Palais 93 25 18 31 www.palais.mc 09.30–18.30
May–Sept; 10.30–17.30 Oct; 10.30–18.00 Apr; closed Nov–Mar

TAKING A BREAK

Le Cappuccino £ ❶ An Italian coffee bar and tea room for snacks and
light lunches. Next to the place du Casino. 5 impasse de la Fontaine
93 25 12 30 07.30–19.00

Crêperie du Rocher £ ❷ This crêperie and pizzeria is a very good lunch
choice in the Old Town. 12 rue Comte Félix Gastaldi 93 30 09 64
11.30–23.00

Lina's Sandwiches £ ❸ Salads and sandwiches in the Métropole
shopping centre. 17 avenue des Spélugues 93 25 86 10
09.00–19.30 Mon–Sat

Café de Paris ££ ❹ It's part of the Monte-Carlo experience, whether
you try the surprisingly good food or just enjoy a drink. Place du Casino
98 06 76 23 Open late for drinks

Quai des Artistes ££ ❺ With a view of the harbour, tables outside and
a traditional brasserie interior. Very good quality, especially the seafood.
Impeccable service and good-value lunch set menu. Between lunch and
dinner times, you can buy drinks. 4 quai Antoine 1er 97 97 97 77
Food served 12.00–14.30 & 19.30–23.00

AFTER DARK

Restaurants

Rampoldi £–££ ❻ An established local favourite serving good Italian
food. 2 avenue des Spélugues 93 30 70 65 12.00–14.00 &
19.30–23.30

Stars N Bars £–££ ❼ On three floors and a magnet for many. Kids are welcome. The upstairs club features live bands. American and Tex-Mex food. ❸ 6 quai Antoine ❶ 97 97 95 95 ❺ 10.00–05.00 July & Aug; 11.00–24.00 Mon–Thur, 11.00–02.00 Fri–Sun, Sept–June

Zebra Square ££–£££ ❽ Trendy and hi-tech, with contemporary Provençal cuisine. Also a lounge bar, with music from 22.00. ❸ Grimaldi Forum, 10 avenue Princesse Grace ❶ 99 99 25 50 ❺ 12.00–04.00

Jöel Robuchon £££ ❾ Master chef Jöel Robuchon's inspiring restaurant at the stunning and luxurious Métropole hotel (recently refurbished, with a fine spa) is a revelation. Open kitchen and superb light dishes impeccably served by friendly staff in a refined ambience. ❸ 4 avenue de la Madone ❶ 93 15 15 10 ❶ Jacket preferred for men

Louis XV £££ ❿ At the plush Hôtel de Paris. This is still chef Alain Ducasse's best restaurant (although he jets to his other projects around the world these days), with a period dining room, a fine terrace and top-quality modern takes on Provençal cuisine. ❸ Place du Casino ❶ 98 06 88 64

Bars, pubs & clubs
Jimmy'z ⓫ The legendary night-club queen Regine founded Jimmy'z at Le Sporting Club de Monaco, and it's still one of the most happening places in town, at steep prices. ❸ Avenue Princesse Grace ❶ 92 16 22 77 ❺ 23.30 onwards Wed–Sun; closed Nov–Easter

Karément ⓬ A cocktail and tapas bar with a terrace and dance floor. ❸ Grimaldi Forum, 10 avenue Princesse Grace ❶ 99 99 20 20 ❿ www.karement.mc ❺ 09.00–04.30

McCarthy's ⓭ A friendly Irish pub with live music and a disco. ❸ 7 rue du Portier ❶ 93 25 87 67 ❺ 18.00–05.00; closed Sun–Wed in winter

⬤ *The magnificent casino was built in 1863 in* belle époque *style*

Roquebrune

Roquebrune, above the Grande Corniche (the highest of the three Corniche roads), is one of the finest hill villages on the Côte d'Azur. Stairways and a warren of narrow alleys lead you upwards. The rue Moncollet, with its medieval houses and covered passageways, is particularly appealing. Once you get to the top, you can get sensational views from the turret of the oldest castle in France. The lovingly restored village has craft and souvenir shops.

Below the village, the forested peninsula of Cap-Martin, with its fine private villas, is yet another haunt of the wealthy. The architect Le Corbusier lived there, and his beach hut, Le Cabanon, is open to the public. The coastal path at the foot of the peninsula is an attractive place for a walk. There is also a modern coastal resort on the cape, with good man-made beaches, near the train station.

THINGS TO SEE & DO

Château de Roquebrune (Roquebrune Castle)
Originally built in the 10th century to defend against Saracen invasions, the castle later became a stronghold of the Grimaldis. In the 1920s it was owned by the Englishman Sir William Ingram. Its four floors (including a dungeon) contain a few exhibits such as arms and furniture.
● Place William Ingram ❶ 04 93 35 07 22 ❷ 10.00–12.30 & 15.00–19.30 July & Aug; 10.00–12.30 & 14.00–18.30 Apr–June & Sept; 10.00–12.30 & 14.00–18.00 Feb, Mar & Oct; 10.00–12.30 & 14.00–17.00 Nov–Jan
❶ Admission charge

TAKING A BREAK

Fraise et Chocolat £ Just at the entrance to the village, a charming tea room serving cakes and other light dishes. ● 1 rue Raymond Poincaré ❶ 06 67 08 32 20 ❷ 09.00–21.00 (summer); 09.00–18.00 (winter); closed late Nov–early Dec

La Grotte £ Good for grills, pasta, seafood or just a drink. ❷ Place des Deux Frères ❶ 04 93 28 99 00 ❹ Food served 12.00–14.30, 19.00–22.00; closed Wed & Nov

Hôtel des Deux Frères ££ Good regional food on a very attractive terrace. ❷ Place des Deux Frères ❶ 04 93 28 99 00 ❹ Closed Sun dinner, Mon, Tues lunch & mid-Nov–mid-Dec

⬤ *Roquebrune, perched on a steep hillside*

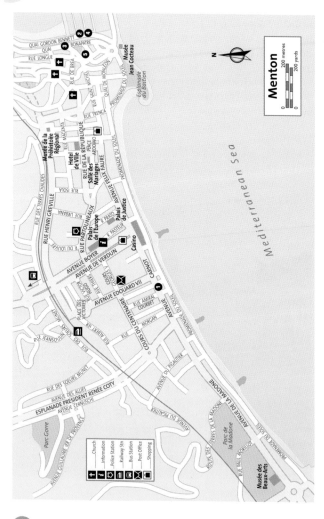

Menton

0 — 200 metres
0 — 200 yards

Mediterranean Sea

Quai Gordon Bennett
Quai Bonaparte
Rue Longue
Rue de Bréa
Rue Saint Michel
Quai de Monléon
Musée Jean Cocteau
Esplanade du Bastion
Promenade du Soleil
Rue Trenca
Rue Magenta
Musée de la Préhistoire Régional
Place Ardoino
Rue de la République
Hôtel de Ville
Salle des Mariages
Rue Isola
Avenue Félix Faure
Rue des Terres Chaudes
Rue Henri Greville
Rue Urbain
Rue Partouneaux
Rue du Louvre
Palais de l'Europe
Rue Pasteur
E Prato
Palais de Justice
Casino
Avenue Boyer
Avenue de Verdun
Cours Cocci
Rue des Tilleuls
Place des Victoires
Avenue Édouard VII
Rue Amiral Courbet
Rue Albert Ier
Rue Morgan
Cours du Centenaire
Avenue Carnot
Promenade du Soleil
Rue Cours Munet
Rue Jeansoulin
Rue des Soeurs Munet
Avenue des Allies
Esplanade Président Renée Coty
Avenue Cernuschi
Avenue du Pigautier
Parc Corre
Avenue Guillaume
Avenue de la Madone
Parc de la Madone
Promenade du Soleil
Rue Mont
Musée des Beaux-Arts

Church
Information
Police Station
Railway Stn
Bus Station
Post Office
Shopping

58

Menton

Very near the Italian border, Menton is one of the most attractive and mellow resorts in the area. Because its sheltered position also makes it one of the warmest, it is famous for its luxuriant gardens, plants and fruits, lemons in particular. Citrus trees grow on steep terraces behind the town. Menton was part of the Grimaldi fiefdom until 1860, when it was ceded to France. But before that, in the 1850s, it became a winter haunt of British and European aristocrats thanks to a book by an English doctor, Henry Bennet, praising its climate. Soon, palace hotels sprang up and a colony of up to 5,000 British lived in the town, which even received a visit from Queen Victoria. Most of the grand, *belle époque* hotels have disappeared now, mostly converted to apartments, and there is an air of faded glory about the place. This doesn't detract from its refined charm, however, which appeals to well-heeled French and Italian visitors. Though many also retire here, it remains a lively place.

Among its attractions are the wide bay, the handsome, palm-lined promenade du Soleil, the beaches, marina, and the pretty, pedestrianised Vieux Menton (Old Menton Town) rising up behind the bustling Vieux Port (old harbour) with its restaurants and cafés. The main thoroughfares of modern Menton are the avenues Verdun and Boyer, divided by the Jardins Biovès.

For luxury shopping head to the area around avenue Félix Faure, and the avenue Verdun. You'll also find boutiques and craft shops in the Old Town. There are several gardens you can visit, both public and private, though some are on the outskirts of town.

There are also several events throughout the year, many of a horticultural nature, but also music festivals of various kinds. The highlight is the famous Lemon Festival in February.

Menton extends to the east into an area of luxurious villas called Garavan. Some of these are open to the public and there is also a very smart marina here.

To the west of the town begin the three spectacular Corniche roads, set one above the other and all with breathtaking views over the Mediterranean. They stretch for over 30 km (19 miles) as far as Nice.

The highest road, the Grande Corniche, was built by Napoleon on the route of the Roman Via Julia Augusta. It rises up to 450 m (490 yds) above Monaco. The middle road, the Moyenne Corniche, was the most recently constructed of the three and it was here that Princess Grace of Monaco had her fatal accident in 1982.

BEACHES

Menton has good beaches; all have showers and are disinfected in summer on a daily basis. There is even a purifying station underground to maintain high water quality for swimmers. Dogs are allowed on only two beaches.

Most of the beaches are private and charge a fee, but you can hire a sun lounger and enjoy bar service and a handy beachfront restaurant. The gravelly Plage des Sabletttes, by the old port, is public.

THINGS TO SEE & DO

Musée des Beaux-Arts (Fine Arts Museum)
This 18th-century building, once the summer palace of the princes of Monaco, is set in a magnificent citrus garden and contains paintings from the 14th century onwards, including some modern works.
ⓐ Palais Carnolès, 3 avenue de la Madone ⓣ 04 93 35 49 71
ⓛ 10.00–12.00 & 14.00–18.00 Wed–Mon

Musée Jean Cocteau (Jean Cocteau Museum)
A small museum in the 17th-century harbour bastion. Founded in 1957, it has paintings, stage sets and other works by the celebrated painter, writer and film director Jean Cocteau, who spent his last years in Menton.
ⓐ Vieux Port ⓣ 04 93 57 72 30 ⓛ 10.00–12.30 & 14.00–18.00 Wed–Mon
ⓘ Admission charge

⬥ One of the pretty gardens in Menton town centre

Salle des Mariages (Wedding Hall)

This hall can be found in Menton's pretty 17th-century town hall. It was decorated with amazing allegorical wall paintings in the 1950s by Jean Cocteau.

ⓐ 17 rue de la République ⓞ 04 92 10 50 29 ⓛ 08.00–12.30 & 14.00–17.00 Mon–Fri ⓘ Admission charge

TAKING A BREAK

Restaurants & bars

There are attractive restaurants and bars along the promenade du Soleil, around the old harbour, and just inside the Old Town (on the harbour side).

Le Bristol £ ❶ Tea room with good local snacks. ⓐ 24 avenue Carnot ⓞ 04 93 57 54 32

Captain's Corner £ ❷ Bar and café with views of the old harbour. Go for seafood or a drink. ⓐ quai Gordon Bennett ⓞ 04 92 41 04 25

L'Albatross £–££ ❸ A straightforward Provençal bistro with a good range of fish and other dishes. ⓐ 31 quai Bonaparte ⓞ 04 93 35 94 64 ⓛ 12.00–15.00 & 19.30–23.00 (22.00 in winter); closed Mon

Au Pistou £–££ ❹ Family-run restaurant with a terrace, and very good seafood and local specialities. ⓐ 9 quai Gordon Bennett ⓞ 04 93 57 45 89 ⓛ Closed Mon & mid-Nov–mid-Dec

Le Stanley £–££ ❺ Specialising in seafood, with tables outside. Friendly service. ⓐ 6 place du Cap ⓞ 04 93 41 37 22

◉ *The inviting Colombe d'Or in St-Paul de Vence*

EXCURSIONS
Out & about

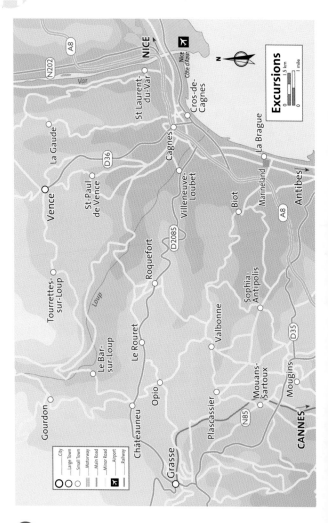

Grasse

Only 17 km (10 miles) northwest of Cannes, Grasse is built on the slopes of a high plateau, surrounded by the flower fields that allow it to call itself the 'world capital of perfume'. The perfume industry was introduced to the town by the queen of France, Catherine de Medici, in the 16th century. The town had previously been known for tanning. Today not only the local flowers, but a vast quantity of imported ones too are used to produce the essences eventually sold to big-name fashion houses and others, and blended to form the world's most famous scents. There are factories around town, some of which are open for visits.

Grasse's sheltered location and fine views made it a popular winter retreat in the 19th century, when visitors included Queen Victoria, and it still attracts many tourists for day trips (particularly since the train from Cannes started running again in 2004), as well as business people attending conferences. Come during the day, though, as there isn't a huge amount of activity at night. You'll find several local dishes served in the restaurants, including *Lou Fassum* (cabbage stuffed with liver and sausage), sweet dishes made with *courge* (marrow), and *fougassette* (brioche made with orange essence).

The somewhat run-down but brightly coloured Old Town has a maze of narrow streets, but the modern town is built in terraces, with long boulevards. Note that Grasse can be a nightmare for drivers, with traffic jams and limited parking. There is, however, a multi-storey car park on cours Honoré Cresp, the main square. The roads from the coast can also get clogged, particularly during rush hour.

THINGS TO SEE & DO

Casino
Pretty much the only venue offering any entertainment after 22.00 in Grasse.

ⓐ Boulevard Jeu de Ballon ⓣ 04 93 36 91 00
ⓦ www.casino-grasse.com

Musée d'Art et d'Histoire de Provence (Provençal Art and History Museum)
This grand 18th-century mansion houses a collection of Provençal art
and artefacts, and gives you a flavour of what it might have been like to
live in the area a couple of centuries ago.
📍 2 rue Mirabeau ☎ 04 93 36 80 20 🌐 www.museesdegrasse.com
🕐 10.00–12.30 & 13.30–18.30 June–Sept; 10.30–12.30 & 14.00–17.00
Wed–Mon, Oct & Dec–May; closed Nov ❶ Admission charge

Musée International de la Parfumerie (International Perfume Museum)
Housed in three fine buildings, the museum charts the history and
production of perfume around the world, as well as soaps, flasks and
bottles, and other articles to do with scent. The greenhouse contains
some of the many plants used in making perfume. The museum is
closed for renovation and is due to re-open in late 2007.
📍 8 cours Honoré Cresp ☎ 04 93 36 80 20 🕐 10.00–19.00 June–Sept;
10.00–12.30 & 14.00–17.00 Wed–Mon, Oct–May ❶ Admission charge

Parfumerie Fragonard & Fabrique des Fleurs
The Fragonard factory (named after the famous locally born painter) lies
in the heart of the town, and here you can discover how perfumes are
made. There's also a small shop and a museum and free daily guided
tours.
    The **Galimard** (📍 73 route de Cannes ☎ 04 93 09 20 00) and **Molinard**
(📍 60 boulevard Victor Hugo ☎ 04 93 36 01 62) factories have similar
hours. Visit on weekdays, when factory staff are at work.
📍 20 boulevard Fragonard ☎ 04 93 36 44 65 🌐 www.fragonard.com
🕐 09.00–18.00 Feb–Oct; 09.00–12.00 & 14.00–18.00 Nov–Jan

TAKING A BREAK

Le Celtic £ A bar and tea room with outdoor tables on the square, serving
snacks, ice cream and more substantial dishes. 📍 4 cours Honoré Cresp
☎ 04 93 36 06 78 🕐 06.30–20.30; closed early Jan

○ *Perfume has been made here since 1782, when this factory was built*

Café des Musées £–££ Modern design and a pleasant ambience, very near the Fragonard factory. You can come for a coffee, *pâtisserie* or something more filling. There's also a small terrace. ❸ 1 rue Jean Ossola ❶ 04 92 60 99 00 ❻ Closed Sun in winter

Le Gazan £–££ A local favourite, with a 'Menu Parfum' in which the food is infused with herbs and other fragrant ingredients. Traditional dishes and a terrace. ❸ 3 rue Gazan ❶ 04 93 36 22 88 ❻ Closed mid-Dec–Feb

Hôtel du Patti £–££ Excellent and well-presented traditional local food in the restaurant (with a terrace) of this small and comfortable hotel. You can also go there for a drink. ❸ Place du Patti ❶ 04 93 36 01 00 ❻ Closed Sun

Lou Fassum ££ Popular restaurant serving Provençal food. ❸ 5 rue des Fabreries ❶ 04 93 42 99 69 ❻ Closed Sun & Mon

⬤ *Perfume vats at the Fragonard factory*

Mougins

Perfectly restored, Mougins still has considerable rustic charm but is one of the most chic and sophisticated hill villages in the whole of Provence. Just 7 km (4 miles) north of Cannes, it's full of the homes of movers and shakers. People come here to eat (it is one of the most famous gastronomic spots in France), play golf, or enjoy the increasingly built-up countryside around it. Others come for the day simply to experience its well-groomed ambience and views.

Fortified in the Middle Ages, Mougins started to attract visitors in the 19th century. In the 20th century, artists of the stature of Picasso, Cocteau, Léger and Man Ray also stayed there. And today many less exalted artists also flock to this spot and have studios and displays in galleries. There are also some excellent (though expensive) food shops and a number of cookery courses on offer.

THINGS TO SEE & DO

Musée de l'Automobiliste (Automobile Museum)

Built in 1984, 5 km (3 miles) east of Mougins, the glossy, modern museum sits just off the A8 motorway, opposite the Aire des Bréguières rest area. It houses one of Europe's finest collections of classic cars (over 100) from 1894 to the present day. A must for car nuts.

ⓐ 772 chemin de Font-de-Carrault ☏ 04 93 69 27 80
ⓦ www.musauto.fr.st ⓛ 10.00–18.00 June–Sept; 10.00–13.00 & 14.00–18.00 Tues–Sun, Oct–May ⓘ Admission charge

Musée de la Photographie (Museum of Photography)

A collection of old photographic equipment, photos of Mougins itself, and work by some of France's greatest photographers, including Jacques Henri Lartigue and Robert Doisneau, all housed in a pleasant, three-storey building. There are also regular temporary exhibitions of contemporary photography.

● *Mougins' pretty streets*

ⓐ Porte Sarrazine ⓣ 04 93 75 85 67 ⓛ 10.00–18.00 Mon–Fri, 11.00–18.00 Sat, Sun & public holidays, Dec–June & Oct; 10.00–20.00 July–Sept; closed Nov

TAKING A BREAK

L'Abreuvoir de Mougins £ Snacks, drinks, ice cream and pastries during the day, and a piano bar at night. Fine views from the terrace. ⓐ 32 place des Patriotes ⓣ 04 93 90 03 05

L'Amandier £–££ Originally owned by Roger Vergé of Moulin de Mougins fame, this immensely pretty restaurant and café in a 14th-century building is very good value for the quality of cooking. Best to book. ⓐ Place des Patriotes ⓣ 04 93 90 00 91

AFTER DARK

Le Mas Candille £££ Set in large grounds, and with great views of the coast, this luxury hotel has one of the finest restaurants in the area. Superb food in very refined surroundings. (See photograph on page 85.) ⓐ Boulevard Clement-Rebuffel ⓣ 04 92 28 43 43

Moulin de Mougins £££ Not actually in the old village but on the road from Cannes, this is one of the most famous restaurants in France, opened in an old olive mill by Roger Vergé in 1969 and handed over to Alain Llorca, formerly at the Negresco in Nice, in 2004. Llorca intensifies flavours in a remarkable way, and his beautifully presented food is cooked in a menu of modern, classic and light Mediterranean dishes. ⓐ Quartier Notre-Dame-de-Vie ⓣ 04 93 75 78 24 ⓛ Closed Mon

Vence

In the foothills of the Alps, 300 m (1,000 ft) above sea level, Vence (and the lovely countryside behind it) provides a refreshing contrast to the bustling coast, though it has plenty of visitors and is only 16 km (10 miles) inland from Nice airport.

Vence was founded as a tribal settlement well before the Romans conquered it in 16 BC (they called it Vintium), and flourished as a result of its strategic location. You can see relics of the Roman occupation in the town even today. It later became a bishopric, and was heavily fortified in the Middle Ages. The oval-shaped Old Town, with its concentric street plan and 13th-century ramparts (entered through five gateways), is the hub of the city and by far its most attractive area. In the bustling alleys near the 17th-century château and the 15th-century Peyra gateway you will find boutiques and shops selling antiques and craft goods, including local pottery. The place du Peyra, the former Roman forum, has an impressive, urn-shaped fountain. But modern Vence is also pleasant, particularly the place du Grand Jardin just outside the Old Town, where you'll find many cafés.

In the 1920s, Vence's fine light and soothing climate became a magnet for artists (including Chagall, Dufy and Soutine) and writers such as D H Lawrence, who died there in 1930. Vence is also famous for fine dining. And the Pays Vençois, the countryside leading into the Alps, is great for walks, drives, vineyard visits or bike rides. There are events in the town throughout the year. A market takes place in the place Clemenceau every morning, near the fine, much-restored 11th-century cathedral.

THINGS TO SEE & DO

Cathédrale Notre-Dame de la Nativité

Built in Merovingian and Romanesqe styles on the site of a Roman temple of Mars, there is a beautiful mosaic by Chagall in the baptistery which shows Moses in the bulrushes.

ⓐ Place Clémenceau ⓑ 09.00–18.00 Mon–Sun

Chapelle du Rosaire (Matisse Chapel)

The chapel is one of the most popular attractions in Vence, and quite rightly; it is simple but exquisite. It was created by Matisse in 1948–51, and he considered it his finest work. Although the painter was an agnostic, he designed the chapel as thanks for being nursed by the Dominican nuns in the neighbouring convent. Light pours through the blue, yellow and green stained-glass window on to the white walls, and the whole effect is uplifting. The simple black designs on the walls depict the Stations of the Cross.

🅐 466 avenue Henri Matisse (route de St-Jeannet) 🕿 04 93 58 21 10
🕔 10.00–11.30 & 14.00–17.30 Tues & Thur; 14.00–17.30 Mon, Wed & Sat
(also Fri during school holidays); closed mid-Nov–mid-Dec
🅘 Admission charge

Château de Villeneuve – Fondation Émile Hugues (Modern Art Museum)

The 15th-century castle of the Villeneuve family, lords of Vence, with its 13th-century watchtower, is now a museum displaying the works of modern artists (such as Matisse and Chagall) associated with Vence, as well as much more contemporary work.

🅐 2 place du Frêne 🕿 04 93 58 15 78 🕔 10.00–18.00 Tues–Sun, July–Oct;
10.00–12.30 & 14.00–18.00 Tues–Sun, Nov–June 🅘 Admission charge

TAKING A BREAK

Bar de L'Etoile £ Traditional cuisine. 🅐 204 avenue des Poilus
🕿 04 93 58 25 81

Crêperie Bretonne £ Serving crêpes and other light dishes in the Old Town. It has a lively terrace. 🅐 6 place Surian 🕿 04 93 24 08 20
🕔 Closed Wed evening & Thur in winter, & Jan

Le Pêcheur du Soleil £ A huge range of high-quality pizzas in the old town. There's a terrace in summer. 🅐 1 place Godeau 🕿 04 93 58 32 56
🕔 Closed Sun & Mon off-season, Dec & Jan

● *The Old Town of Vence*

Brasserie La Victoire £–££ A typical brasserie, with tables outside.
ⓐ Place du Grand Jardin ① 04 93 24 21 15

Auberge des Seigneurs ££ Provençal specialities, particularly grilled meat, in a 17th-century building. ⓐ Place du Frêne ① 04 93 58 04 24
Ⓛ Closed Mon, Tues–Thur lunch, & mid-Nov–mid-Dec

Le Vieux Couvent ££ In the chapel of a 17th-century convent, serving excellent regional dishes made with the freshest ingredients.
ⓐ 37 avenue Alphonse Toreille ① 04 93 58 78 58

L'Auberge des Templiers ££–£££ Top-quality modern Mediterranean food served in the garden in good weather. ⓐ 30 avenue Joffre
① 04 93 58 06 05

Table d'Amis de Jacques Maximin £££ Jacques Maximin is about the most famous chef in Provence, and this superb gastronomic restaurant won't disappoint if you want the highest-quality cuisine. You can eat in the garden in good weather, or in the splendid restaurant.
ⓐ 689 chemin de la Gaude ① 04 93 58 90 Ⓛ Closed Mon, Sun dinner, & mid-Nov–mid-Dec

St-Paul de Vence

One of the most fashionable and visited hill villages in the region, St-Paul itself is exceptionally pretty, but the attractive view, once splendid, is now somewhat spoilt by the proliferation of villas in the valley below. The main sight is the fortified village itself, with its winding streets, pretty little squares and small art galleries (of varying quality), and shops selling crafts and souvenirs. Tourist Information will give you a full list of shops. The main street, the rue Grande, runs through the village and is the first place to head for. You can also walk most of the way along the 16th-century ramparts.

St-Paul attracted many of the great artists of the 20th century; at the entrance of the village is the famous Colombe d'Or hotel, whose walls are covered by a collection of modern art which most museums would kill for, all donated by artists of the calibre of Matisse, Picasso and Braque in return for free board and lodging. Many major celebrities also stay there. It's best to arrive early to find a space in one of the car parks at the village entrance. There is a Provençal market near the boule pitch at the foot of the town every morning except Fridays and Sundays. St-Paul is 20 km (12 miles) west of Nice.

THINGS TO SEE & DO

Église Collégiale (Collegiate Church)
At the top of the village, the 12th–13th-century church houses some important art works, and has a captivating interior.
ⓐ Place de l'Église ⓕ 08.00–20.00

Fondation Maeght
Just outside St-Paul, this is one of the finest modern art galleries in France, founded by art dealer Aimé Maeght in 1964, and now visited by 250,000 people a year. Not only are the exhibits notable, but also the setting and the building itself, designed by the Spanish architect J L Sert.

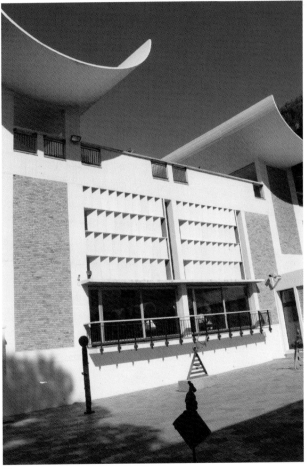

● *Fondation Maeght: modern art in a Modernist building*

⬤ *The* boule *pitch in St-Paul de Vence*

As well as the regular collection, the museum holds major special exhibitions. There is a good bookshop and café. It's about 500 m (550 yards) from the village entrance, not far from the first parking area.

🚌 Chemin des Trious ☎ 04 93 32 81 63 🌐 www.fondationmaeght.com
🕐 10.00–19.00 July–Sept; 10.00–12.30 & 14.30–18.00 Oct–June
ℹ Admission charge

Musée d'Histoire Locale (Local History Museum)

A 16th-century house, refurbished in period style, retraces the history of St-Paul, with wax figures in period costumes.

🚌 Place de l'Église ☎ 04 93 32 41 13 🕐 10.00–19.30 summer; 10.00–17.00 winter; closed mid-Nov–mid-Dec ℹ Admission charge

Musée de Saint-Paul

A permanent collection of modern and contemporary art, with some temporary exhibitions.

🚌 2 rue Grande ☎ 04 93 32 86 95 🕐 10.00–19.00 summer; 10.00–18.00 winter

TAKING A BREAK

La Terrasse sur Saint-Paul £ Salads, pizza, ice cream and crêpes served on a large terrace with a sea view. 🚌 20 chemin des Trious ☎ 04 93 32 85 60 🕐 Closed Wed

Café de la Place £–££ Just by the boule pitch at the foot of the village, this café, with a terrace and mirrored interior reminiscent of Parisian brasseries, is an excellent choice for lunch or a drink. 🚌 Place de Gaulle ☎ 04 93 32 80 03 🕐 07.00–24.00 summer; 07.00–20.00 winter; closed Nov–mid-Dec

La Terrasse £–££ Enjoy crêpes, salads and Provençal dishes on the terrace. ⓐ 66 rue Grande ⓣ 04 93 32 02 05 ⓛ 11.30–18.00

Hostellerie Les Remparts ££ Accomplished Provençal dishes, salads and grills served in a restaurant and on a terrace with good views. ⓐ 72 rue Grande ⓣ 04 93 32 09 88 ⓛ 12.00–15.00 & 19.30–21.30; closed Tues dinner & Wed

La Colombe d'Or ££–£££ One of the most famous spots on the coast, yet the set lunch (assuming you can get a table) is quite reasonably priced for the quality of the simple food and the status of the hotel. You can eat inside in the restaurant with its famous paintings, or on the sunny terrace. Or just go for a drink. ⓐ Place de Gaulle ⓣ 04 93 32 80 02 ⓛ Closed Nov, Dec & part of Jan

Le Saint-Paul £££ The best hotel in the village itself serves refined Provençal cuisine either in the vaulted dining room or on the flowery terrace. ⓐ 86 rue Grande ⓣ 04 93 32 65 25 ⓛ 12.30–13.45 & 19.45–21.45; closed Tues & Wed lunch Oct–Apr

◗ *Enjoying the sun at the Nice cafés*

Food & drink

The Côte d'Azur is part of Provence and the local cuisine is essentially Provençal, with a strong emphasis on regional ingredients such as olive oil (which is used instead of butter for cooking), garlic, lamb, game, tomatoes, olives, artichokes, aubergines, fennel and herbs such as rosemary, lavender, thyme and basil. Meat is often grilled, and the traditional flavours of Provençal food are bold and often intense, but without a great reliance on sauces. And, because of the quality of the vegetables, vegetarians will have a better choice than they would in most of the rest of France. Indeed, a simply dressed tomato salad is one of the pleasures of being in the area. Fruit is also excellent. And *ratatouille* (aubergines, peppers, tomatoes, courgettes and garlic cooked in olive oil), which is a Provençal dish, tastes so much better here than anywhere else. Dishes described as *à la provençal* are normally cooked with tomatoes, oil and garlic.

The cheeses of the region aren't particularly varied and you are most likely to find *chèvre* (goat's milk cheese) on the menu and, in more sophisticated restaurants, cheeses from other parts of France.

The fact that it is a Mediterranean area means that fish and seafood are found on most menus in the Côte d'Azur. The most famous fish dish of the area, originating further west along the coast in Marseille, is *bouillabaisse*. There is much argument about what a real *bouillabaisse* should contain, but experts seem to agree that it should consist of a minimum of four types of fish (which should be as fresh as possible), including *rascasse* (the ugly scorpion fish), John Dory and monkfish. The fish is cooked with onions, saffron, olive oil, garlic, fennel, parsley, potatoes and tomatoes. The dish is traditionally served in two parts; the fish is presented separately from the broth, which is eaten with a garlic mayonnaise called *rouille* and croutons.

As anywhere in France, cafés and brasseries serve traditional staples such as steak and chips, sausages (including the Moroccan lamb sausages called *merguez*), *confit de canard* (conserve of duck), *magret de canard* (breast of duck) and stews.

The cosmopolitan nature of the coast means that menus in restaurants and cafés often feature dishes from around the world. In particular, the coast's proximity to Italy means that Italian dishes are found in many restaurants, particularly pasta and pizzas. Because of France's links to North Africa, you will also find several restaurants serving Moroccan food.

A tempting display of local produce

NICE

Nice has its own distinctive cuisine, with dishes such as *estoficada* (stockfish stew) and *omelette à la poutine* (with sardines and anchovies). *Boeuf à la niçoise* comes with tomatoes and olives, and *agneau à la niçoise* (lamb) is cooked with courgettes, tomatoes and new potatoes. *Ravioli niçoise* is presented with beef stew. Nice's most famous dish has to be the *salade niçoise*. As with *bouillabaisse*, there are arguments about what it should contain, but tomatoes, anchovy fillets (or tuna, or both), olives, onions, green beans and hard-boiled eggs are usual ingredients. Sometimes boiled potatoes are also added. The salad is pretty much a meal in itself.

Nice, and the area around it, is also a good place for interesting snacks, including *pan-bagnat* (basically a *salade niçoise* sandwich), *pissaladière* (a tart, not unlike pizza, baked with a topping of onions, olives and anchovies), *socca* (a pancake made with ground chickpeas) and *fougassette* (a pastry made of brioche dough, which is normally sweet but also comes in savoury versions).

RESTAURANTS

The Côte d'Azur is home to some of the finest restaurants in the world, often found in hotels, and sometimes in spectacular locations.

Whatever type of restaurant you visit, you will find that set menus (assuming you are hungry) offer the best value, particularly at lunchtime. But in cities such as Nice, you will be able to find more modestly priced places catering mainly for locals, as long as you are willing to get off the beaten track.

Most restaurants are open 12.00–14.30 or 15.00 for lunch, and then from 19.00 or 19.30 to 22.30 or 23.00. But simpler brasseries, pizzerias and cafés open much earlier and close after midnight in high season. They are usually open all day. Some restaurants close for a couple of weeks (or more) out of season, so it is always advisable to check, particularly if you want to visit an up-market establishment.

The dress code in most cafés and brasseries tends to be casual, but in more expensive restaurants, smart-casual is the safest option, particularly in the evening.

⬥ *This restaurant in Mougins offers superb views*

Restaurants and cafés in France are required to have separate smoking and non-smoking areas. However, new laws are going to be introduced for restaurants, bars and clubs from early 2008, banning smoking indoors. If you want to eat outside, get to your venue early or book; in good weather, outdoor tables fill up fast.

DRINKS

It's best (and cheapest) to order local wines in bars and restaurants. You'll find Provençal wines very drinkable. The fruity rosé wines the area is famous for are a perfect accompaniment to lighter dishes, particularly seafood. Local whites, though not necessarily the most impressive you will find in France, are dry and improving all the time, and the best are very good with fish. Reds can be full-bodied (especially those from the Rhône valley) but others, such as Bandol, are fruitier. If you want a decent local wine, names to look for are Château Minuty, Château Pibarnon, Bellet, Belieu and Pierrefeu.

Wines served in carafes or *pichets* (jugs) will be the cheapest, and the finest local wines served in bottles, although on the expensive side, will still be cheaper on the whole than good wines from the rest of France.

Apart from wine, the local tipple is *pastis* (usually Ricard or Pernod), flavoured with aniseed and drunk diluted with water and ice. Sometimes pastis is mixed with syrups to produce concoctions such as *perroquet* (with mint), *tomate* (with grenadine) and *mauresque* (with almond and orange syrup). If you prefer beer, it is almost always cheaper to drink French brands, such as Kronenbourg, rather than imported ones. The cheapest is *pression* (draught beer).

TIPPING

Service is included in French restaurants (and bars) of any type, so there is no need to leave a tip unless you feel you have had an exceptionally good experience.

Menu decoder

It's worth noting that some menus in smaller or more traditional places use Provençal terms for various types of food, rather than French. Some of these are given below. That said, many restaurants have menus in English as well as French.

Agneau Lamb
Aigo boulido Garlic soup
Ail Garlic
Aïoli Garlic mayonnaise
Anchoïade Anchovy paste
Anchois Anchovies
Andouillette Chitterling sausage
Asperges Asparagus
Au four Cooked in an oven
Bar Sea bass
Barbue Brill
Basilica Basil
Béarnaise Mayonnaise-type sauce made with tarragon, usually eaten with steak
Bisque Thick shellfish soup
Boeuf Beef
Bouillabaisse Fish stew
Brandade de morue Dip of salt cod, milk and garlic
Cabillaud Cod
Caille Quail
Calamar Squid
Calisson Small almond cake
Canard Duck

Cerise Cherry
Champignon Mushroom
Chèvre or cabro Goat
Choucroute Sauerkraut
Citron Lemon
Civet de lièvre Jugged hare
Confit Meat (usually duck) cooked in its own fat and preserved
Contre-filet Sirloin steak
Coquillages Shellfish
Coquilles St-Jacques Scallops
Cornichon Gherkin
Couscous Moroccan steamed semolina, usually served with lamb or chicken
Crêpe Thin pancake
Crespeou Savoury pancake
Crevettes Prawns
Croque-monsieur Toasted ham and cheese sandwich
Croustade Pastry usually filled with seafood or other savoury contents
Crudités Selection of raw vegetables, usually sliced

Daube Meat slowly cooked in red wine

Dorade Sea bream

Épices Spices

Épinards Spinach

Escargots Snails, usually served with garlic butter and parsley

Espadon Swordfish

Estoficada Stockfish stew

Estragon Tarragon

Farci Stuffed

Fenouil Fennel

Figue Fig

Foie Liver

Fraises Strawberries

Framboises Raspberries

Frites French fries

Fromage Cheese

Fruits de mer Seafood

Fumé Smoked

Galette Pancake made with buckwheat flour

Gambas Large prawns

Gibier Game

Gigot (d'agneau) Leg of lamb

Gingembre Ginger

Glace Ice cream

Haricots verts Green beans

Homard Lobster

Huîtres Oysters

Jambon Ham

Jus Juice or gravy

Laitue Lettuce

Langoustine Dublin Bay prawn

Lapin Rabbit

Lardons Small pieces of bacon

Légumes Vegetables

Lotte Monkfish

Loup de mer Sea bass

Magret Breast of duck

Menthe Mint

Merguez Spicy lamb sausage

Miel Honey

Morue Dried salt cod

Moules Mussels

Moutarde Mustard

Oeuf Egg

Oignons Onions

Oursins Sea urchin

Pain Bread

Palourdes Cockles

Pamplemousse Grapefruit

Pâte Usually pasta, but also pastry

Pêche Peach

Persil Parsley

Petits-fours Small sweets and cakes, usually served at the end of the meal with coffee

Pignons Pine nuts

Pintade Guineafowl

Pissaladière Pizza-like onion tart with anchovy

Pistou Provençal vegetable soup with garlic, basil and olive oil

Poireaux Leaks

Pois Peas

Poisson Fish

Pomme Apple

Pomme de terre Potato

Pot-au-feu Boiled meat, served with its broth

Potage Soup

Poulet Chicken

Poulpe Octopus (also **pourpre** in Provençal)

Prune Plum

Quenelle Mousse of fish or white meat

Ragoût Stew

Raie Skate

Raisins Grapes

Ratatouille Provençal dish of aubergine, tomatoes, peppers, courgettes and garlic

Rilettes Potted, shredded pork

Ris de veau Calf sweetbreads

Riz Rice

Rognons Kidneys

Romarin Rosemary

Rôti Roast

Rouget Red mullet

Rouille Hot garlic mayonnaise served with fish soups

Safran Saffron

St-Pierre John Dory

Salade niçoise Salad of tomatoes, tuna, anchovies, beans and olives

Sanglier Wild boar

Saucisse Singular sausage

Saucisson Salami-type sausage

Sauge Sage

Saumon Salmon

Socca Chickpea pancake

Supion Small squid

Suprême de volaille Chicken breast

Tapenade Olive, oil and garlic purée, often served before a meal

Terrine Coarse pâté

Thon Tuna

Thym Thyme

Tranche Slice

Truffes Truffles

Truite Trout

Vapeur Steamed

Veau Veal

Viande Meat

Volaille Poultry

Shopping

The Côte d'Azur offers shopping of all types from international designer stores to chain stores, as well as street markets and shops selling local specialities. But apart from food and drink, mass-market clothes and the odd craft item, you'll do well to find a bargain.

The main local craft specialities to look for are ceramics and pottery, perfume, soap (hand-made with oil and in a large range of scents and colours), glassware, wood sculptures and weaving. Some villages specialise in particular crafts. Brightly coloured Provençal fabrics, particularly those in a paisley pattern, are well known. In the markets, you will find them sold by the metre, as well as covering cushions, bags of lavender and bread baskets, among other objects. The most internationally famous outlets for Provençal fabrics are Souleiado and Olivades. Both companies have shops in many of the coast's resorts.

As for food items, the local olives (and the olive paste *tapenade*), dried herbs, goat's cheese, honey, *saucisson* (dry, salami-type sausage), and confectionery such as nougat and *calissons* (small almond cakes), are all worth taking back home. Above all, rich and fruity Provençal olive oil, among the finest in the world, is a must-buy. The *huile vierge extra* (cold-pressed extra virgin oil) is best for dressings, while the *huile vierge* is the highest-quality cooking oil.

Wine and other forms of alcohol are substantially cheaper in France than in Britain. Wine is best bought in specialist shops or supermarkets, but if you decide to go on a wine tour, you can purchase from the vineyard shops themselves.

Everywhere you go, you will find *boulangeries* (bakeries), which sell small snacks such as mini pizzas as well as bread, *pâtisseries* (pastry shops), *épiceries fines* (delicatessens) and *épiceries* (small groceries), many selling high-quality products. Although most resorts have small supermarkets, only the largest have full-scale supermarkets and these are often on the outskirts of town. They will offer a large range of goods including clothing and electrical items. You should have no difficulty finding shops selling items for the beach, even in the smallest resort.

Pot Pourri
5 euros
le Sachet

Pick your scent from this colourful selection

In Nice, the main shopping streets are the avenue Jean-Médicin and the pedestrianised rue Masséna. The rue Masséna is full of boutiques, while department stores such as Galeries Lafayette are around the place Masséna. For top designers' clothes shops, go to the rue Paradis. The Nice-Étoile development on avenue Jean-Médicin also houses a number of major stores and has a car park. In the Old Town you will find food, gift and craft shops. There is a Carrefour hypermarket just north of Nice airport, and the giant Cap 3000 shopping centre is west of the airport at St-Laurent-du-Var. Note that shops at Nice airport are generally more expensive for food, souvenirs and alcohol than in the city itself.

Monaco is a paradise if you like luxury goods at luxurious prices. Go to the area around the casino, the place du Casino and avenue de Monte-Carlo, for leading names in clothes and jewellery, such as Vuitton, Bulgari, Van Cleef and Arpels, Hermès, Dior and Chanel. The Metropole shopping centre is also nearby. The other main shops are around the boulevard des Moulins and rue Grimaldi. The Centre Commercial in Fontvieille is a shopping centre with a hypermarket.

Cannes is another heaven for serious shopaholics. The smartest shops are on La Croisette, on the rue d'Antibes, and in the streets in between. For traditional food and craft shops, head for the rue Meynardier and the streets around it in the old port.

MARKETS

Antibes The fish, fruit and vegetable market is in cours Masséna every morning except Monday.

Cannes The covered Forville market is open Tues–Sat. It is a bric-à-brac market on Mondays.

Grasse There is a daily food and flower market in cours Honoré Cresp. A one-day truffle market takes place in mid-January.

Menton An indoor market is held daily on quai de Monléon near the Cocteau Museum, and there's a street market near the bus station.

Nice There is a flower, fruit and vegetable market in cours Saleya every day except Monday, when there is a flea market.

Children

Children are generally welcome in France, and the Côte d'Azur is no exception. The majority of hotels will normally be very helpful if you are travelling with small children. And most restaurants, particularly cafés and brasseries, gladly serve them. Indeed, many simpler places offer a *menu enfant* (children's menu). Only the grandest places may not be so welcoming, but even here it is perfectly normal to see well-behaved teenagers eating, although not infants. You will find plenty of food on sale that will appeal to them, such as *steak haché* (minced steak patties), pasta, pizzas, *pissaladière*, ice cream and Provençal pastes and dips such as *tapenade* and *brandade*. Chips are ubiquitous, and even a *salade niçoise* might appeal to many children. If they really miss the fast food of home, they won't have to go without, as McDonald's and other chains, shunned in much of France, have sprung up in most resorts.

If you need baby supplies such as baby food and nappies, you might have to seek out a large supermarket, as smaller pharmacies do not often stock these items.

Beaches apart, the Côte d'Azur has a surprisingly large range of activities and attractions that children might not actually have to be dragged to.

Antibes
The Marineland theme and adventure park (see page 24) should appeal to children of all ages, not to mention adults. There is also the Naval & Napoleonic Museum (see page 25).

Grasse
Older children might enjoy a visit to the International Perfume Museum or one of the perfume factories open to the public (see page 66).

Monaco
Full of attractions such as the Oceanographic Museum & Aquarium (see page 52), Classic Car Collection (see page 50), zoo (see page 50) and

National Museum of Automata & Dolls (see page 52). For more active pursuits, visit the Parc Princesse Antoinette, which has a playground and mini-golf (🄐 54 bis boulevard du Jardin Exotique 🄓 10.00–12.00 & 14.00–18.00). At the Mini-Club de la Plage du Larvotto there are organised activities for children aged 3–10 in July and August (🄐 Avenue Princesse Grace 🄓 Mon–Fri). The Azur Express tourist train might also appeal (🄐 Musée Océanographique, avenue St-Martin 🄣 92 05 64 38 🄓 10.00–17.00 summer; 10.30–18.00 winter; closed Jan & mid-Nov–26 Dec 🄘 Admission charge, but children under five free).

● *There are plenty of places for kids to play*

Mougins
Don't miss the glitzy Automobile Museum (see page 69), outside the village off the A8.

Nice
Children should enjoy a ride on the 'Petit Train Touristique' (⊜ Promenade des Anglais, opposite Jardin Albert 1er ⊙ 04 93 62 85 48 ⊙ 10.00–20.00 summer; 10.00–18.00 winter; closed mid-Nov–mid-Jan). Similar trains also run in all the main towns. Also try a visit to the Castel des Deux Rois amusement park (see page 32) or the Natural History Museum (see page 33).

Roquebrune
Children will enjoy a trip to Roquebrune Castle (see page 56) and its dungeon.

St-Jean-Cap-Ferrat
The Zoo-Parc Cap-Ferrat (see page 44) is small but lots of fun for kids.

Villefranche-sur-Mer
The Citadelle St-Elme (see page 40) will keep the little ones occupied for a while.

> **BEING SUN-SMART**
> Particularly when you have children with you, you need to guard against the strong sun in summer, and insect bites. You should have no difficulty finding sun creams and insect repellents in the many local pharmacies.

Sports & activities

CYCLING

Cycling is, of course, a major competitive sport in France, but if you simply want to hire a bike for a gentle ride, you will have no trouble finding hire shops along the coast. You can also hire bikes at some railway stations such as Antibes and Cannes. And there are several designated mountain bike paths near hill towns such as Mougins.

GOLF

Although there are a number of mini-golf places dotted around the coast, serious golfers also have plenty of choice, and you can hire equipment from most of the clubs mentioned below.

⬤ *Hire a bike or go for a skate along a sunny promenade*

Grasse

Golf Country Club de Saint-Donat Green fees are around €51–€75.
ⓐ 270 route de Cannes, 06130 Grasse ⓣ 04 93 09 76 60 ⓕ 04 93 09 76 63
ⓦ www.golfsaintdonat.com

Golf du Claux-Amic With fine views and green fees of around €60.
ⓐ 1 route des 3 Ponts, Lieu-dit Claux Amic, 06130 Grasse ⓣ 04 93 60 55 44
ⓕ 04 93 60 55 19 ⓦ www.claux-amic.com

Monte-Carlo

Monte-Carlo Golf Club Spectacularly situated, 900 m (2,953 ft) up in the hills behind the city. There is also a practice range. Green fees are around €90–€110. ⓐ Route de Mont Agel, 06320 La Turbie ⓣ 04 92 41 50 70
ⓕ 04 93 41 09 55 ⓔ monte-carlo-golf-club@wanadoo.fr

Mougins

Golf Country Club Prestigious, with green fees of around €100–€120.
ⓐ 175 avenue du Golf, 06250 Mougins ⓣ 04 93 75 79 13 ⓕ 04 93 75 27 60
ⓦ www.golf-cannes-mougins.com

Royal Mougins Golf Club Beautifully landscaped and exclusive, opened in 1993, with green fees of around €175–€225 at weekends. ⓐ 424 avenue du Roi, 06250 Mougins ⓣ 04 92 92 49 69 ⓕ 04 92 92 49 70
ⓦ www.royalmougins.fr

Nice

Golf Country Club de Nice A nine-hole course outside Nice. ⓐ 698 route de Grenoble, 06200 Nice ⓣ 04 93 29 82 00 ⓕ 04 93 29 86 71

GYMS

Most of the grander hotels on the coast have gyms and other fitness facilities, and non-residents are normally able to visit for a fee. The bigger resorts all have gyms and fitness centres, such as the Espace Wellness in Nice. You can pay on a daily or weekly basis.

⬥ The streets of Monte-Carlo, marked out for the Monaco Grand Prix circuit

Espace Wellness ⓐ 11 rue Maccarani ⓣ 04 97 03 14 14 ⓦ www.espace-wellness.fr ⓛ 09.00–21.00 Mon–Fri, 09.00–18.00 Sat

HELICOPTER RIDES

You can take a trip in a helicopter to see Monaco or the rest of the Côte d'Azur from the air. There are also various helicopter packages available, which include other activities. The Monaco trip takes 10–15 minutes, the rest of the coast is an hour-long tour. There must be a minimum of four passengers, and prices start at around €50 per person. It's best to book in advance. Two companies offer trips from the heliport in Fontvieille:

Héli Air Monaco ⓐ Héliport de Monaco, avenue des Ligures ⓣ 92 05 00 50 ⓦ www.heliairmonaco.com ⓜ Bus: 5, 6

Monacair ⓐ Héliport de Monaco, avenue des Ligures ⓣ 97 97 39 00 ⓦ www.monacair.mc

HORSE RIDING

If you venture into the hills behind the coast, you will find several opportunities for riding. Riding clubs include:

Centre Hippique de Mougins With 8 km (5 miles) of marked trails. ⓐ Chemin de Font de Currault, 06250 Mougins ⓣ 04 93 45 75 81 ⓕ 04 93 45 61 25

Club Hippique de Grasse Near Grasse. ⓐ 168 route de Cannes, 06130 Grasse ⓣ 04 93 70 55 41

PARAGLIDING & HANG-GLIDING

You can paraglide near Roquebrune. Check the website of the local paragliding club for more details, particularly the strict regulations (ⓦ www.roquebrunailes.com). You can also contact the Fédération Française de Vol Libre for details of all activities, clubs and events in the area ⓐ 4 rue de Suisse, 0600 Nice ⓣ 04 97 03 82 82 ⓦ www.ffvl.fr

SAILING & BOAT HIRE

With 33 yacht harbours, the Côte d'Azur is one of the best places in the whole Mediterranean for sailing. You should have no trouble hiring most types of boat, with or without crew. Boat trips and tours are also available. Check with local Tourist Information to find out what's on offer. The regional tourist website (ⓦ www.guideriviera.com) carries a list of yacht and boat hire companies and their contact details.

SPAS

You can find spas in most resorts and in almost all the coast's grand hotels (usually also open to non-residents who want to be pampered). There are also several thalassotherapy centres, including the luxurious Thermes Marins in Monaco (ⓐ 2 avenue de Monte-Carlo ⓞ 98 06 68 00 ⓦ www.montecarlospa.com ⓛ 08.00–20.00).

TENNIS

There are tennis courts and clubs throughout the area. Many of the larger hotels have their own courts.

WALKING & JOGGING

There are numerous opportunities for walks. You could, for instance, walk or jog along La Croisette in Cannes or the promenade des Anglais in Nice, or walk up the hill of Le Château or Mont Boron in Nice. The walk up to Èze village from the coast is pretty challenging, and there are also various coastal walks, including the one running from Beaulieu to Cap-Ferrat. The hills behind Vence will appeal to more serious walkers, and you can get maps of marked walks from Tourist Information. Mougins also has marked walking and jogging trails.

WATER SPORTS

If you just want to swim, there are 40 km (25 miles) of beaches on the Côte d'Azur, as well as hotel and public pools. But many other activities are also available, particularly in the bigger resorts. These include scuba diving, waterskiing, windsurfing, parascending, and jet-ski and pedalo hire.

Festivals & events

There are traditional, cultural and sporting events and art shows throughout the year. For full listings, consult your local Tourist Information office or visit the tourism website (ⓦ www.guideriviera.com).

JANUARY

Cannes Shopping Festival. Glitzy fashion and other events during the first week of January, including a classic car parade.
ⓦ www.cannesshoppingfestival.com

Monaco Rally Automobile Monte-Carlo. The famous Monte-Carlo Rally has been going since 1911 and takes place over three days around the

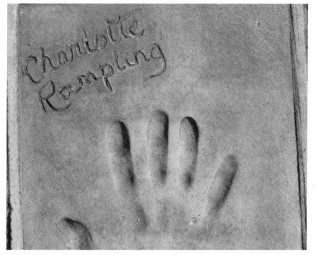

⬤ *The stars leave their mark in Cannes*

middle of January (www.acm.mc). There's also an International
Circus Festival at the end of the month
(www.montecarlofestivals.com).

FEBRUARY
Menton Fête du Citron. Lemon festival with colourful floats.

Nice Carnaval de Nice. The carnival, with its floats and flower parade,
is one of the most colourful and ebullient events on the whole coast
and takes place for two weeks before Lent, with the spectacular
finale on Shrove Tuesday. It draws big crowds.
www.nicecarnaval.com

MARCH
Juan-les-Pins Napoleon's landing in 1815 is re-enacted in nearby Golfe-
Juan.

Nice Festin des Cougourdons. An eccentric folklore festival in late
March/early April celebrating gourds. The vegetables are dried and
decorated.

APRIL
Monaco Monte-Carlo Masters Series. A week of international tennis at
the Monte-Carlo Country Club. www.mcc.mc

MAY
Cannes Film Festival. The world-famous event runs for 12 days in late May.
www.festival-cannes.org

Grasse Rose Festival. www.ville-grasse.fr

Monaco Grand Prix. Held in late May, coinciding with Ascension Day, and
preceded a few days earlier by a series of races for old cars.
www.acm.mc

Nice Fête de Mai. A family festival, with music, dancing and picnics, held in Cimiez on Sundays and holidays throughout the month.
ⓦ www.nicetourisme.com

JUNE

Antibes Voiles d'Antibes. Four-day regatta in early June. ⓘ 93 34 42 47
ⓦ www.voilesdantibes.com

Nice Fête de la Mer. On 29 June, Nice's fishermen celebrate St Peter's feast day in the old port.

JULY

Cannes Antique Show. ⓦ www.antiquaires-contact.com

Juan-les-Pins Jazz à Juan. Top artists appear at this famous jazz festival in mid-July. ⓘ Information 92 90 53 00 ⓦ www.antibesjuanlespins.com

Nice Jazz Festival. Mid-July in the Roman amphitheatre at Cimiez.
ⓘ Tickets 08 92 70 75 07 ⓦ www.nicejazzfest.com

Monaco Festival de la Télévision de Monte-Carlo. International TV festival.
ⓦ www.tvfestival.com

Vence Les Nuits du Sud. Month-long outdoor world music festival running to mid-August. ⓦ www.ville-vence.fr

AUGUST

Grasse Jasmine Festival on the first weekend of the month.
Menton Chamber Music Festival. ⓦ www.villedementon.com

SEPTEMBER

Cannes International Yachting Festival
(ⓦ www.salonnautiquecannes.com), with the Royal Regattas

(Ⓦ www.regatesroyal.com) and Cannes Golf Classic later in the month.
Monaco Yacht Show. ❶ 93 10 41 70 Ⓦ www.monacoyachtshow.com

OCTOBER

Nice Ste-Réparte Festival. Celebration of Nice's patron saint in the Old Town, with religious services, music and dancing.

NOVEMBER

Monaco National Day. 19 November is celebrated with gala performances and a firework display.

DECEMBER

Cannes Festival de Danse. Contemporary dance festival.
Ⓦ www.cannes-on-line.com

❿ *Directions are usually clearly signposted*

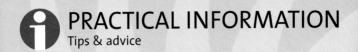

Preparing to go

GETTING THERE

By air

Nice-Côte d'Azur airport serves flights from a number of UK airlines. British Airways has several direct flights a day from Heathrow, and a smaller number from Gatwick and Birmingham. easyJet flights go from Gatwick, Luton, Stansted, Bristol, Liverpool, Newcastle and Belfast. British Midland flies from Heathrow, and Bmibaby from both Birmingham and Heathrow. Aer Lingus flies from Dublin and Cork. The flight time from London is about two hours.

Bmibaby ☎ 0871 224 0224 ⓦ www.bmibaby.com
British Airways ☎ 0870 850 9 850 ⓦ www.ba.com
British Midland ☎ 0870 6070 555 ⓦ www.flybmi.com
easyJet ☎ 0871 244 2366 ⓦ www.easyjet.com

Many people are aware that air travel emits CO_2, which contributes to climate change. You may be interested in the possibility of lessening the environmental impact of your flight through the charity Climate Care, which offsets your CO_2 by funding environmental projects around the world. Visit ⓦ www.climatecare.org

By train

From London (Waterloo at the time of writing, but soon to be St Pancras) you can get to Nice by Eurostar, changing for a TGV at either Paris (where you have to transfer from the Gare du Nord to the Gare de Lyon) or at Lille. The total journey time is around 9–10 hours. From Nice, you can take trains to other destinations along the coast, from Nice-Ville station, St-Augustin station (near the airport), or Riquier station (to the east of the city). The monthly Thomas Cook European Rail Timetable has up-to-date schedules for European international and national train services:

Eurostar reservations UK ☎ 08705 186 186 ⓦ www.eurostar.com
French Railways (SNCF) ⓦ www.sncf.com
Rail Europe ☎ 08705 848 848 ⓦ www.raileurope.co.uk

Thomas Cook European Rail Timetable ❶ (UK) 01733 416477; (USA) 1 800 322 3834 ⓦ www.thomascookpublishing.com

By car

If you drive from the UK, you are best going via Calais. You will take around 10–12 hours to cover the 1,200 km (720 miles) from Calais to Nice, so it's probably less stressful to stop for a night en route. Take the A7 south to Aix-en-Provence and then the A8 *autoroute*. Remember that toll charges apply to these roads, so make sure you have enough euros (or a credit card) on you.

TOURISM INFORMATION

The French Government Tourist Information website will give you the latest information about travelling to France and your destination (ⓦ www.franceguide.com). You can also try the comprehensive Côte d'Azur website (ⓦ www.guideriviera.com). The main towns and cities on

TRAVEL INSURANCE

Visitors from the UK are covered by EU reciprocal health schemes while in France. You should take a European Health Insurance Card (EHIC) with you when you go; this can be obtained free of charge through most UK post offices or through the UK Department of Health via their website (ⓦ www.dh.gov.uk) or by telephoning ❶ 0845 6062030 (from outside the UK call (0044) 191203555). The EHIC is not a substitute for medical and travel insurance, but entitles you to emergency medical treatment on the same terms as French nationals. You will not be covered for medical repatriation, on-going medical treatment or treatment of a non-urgent nature. Always make sure you have adequate travel insurance, covering not only health, but possessions, etc. All non-EU travellers should also make sure they have adequate insurance before they travel.

⬥ *The police are friendlier than they appear*

the Côte d'Azur all have their own websites as well. To track down a business or organisation, try the French Yellow Pages (ⓦ www.pagesjaunes.fr).

BEFORE YOU LEAVE

The Côte d'Azur has a highly developed infrastructure, so you will be able to find everything you need. However, it is sensible to take prescription medicines and items such as contact lens solution with you. Note that many drugs that are widely available in the UK are obtainable only at pharmacies in France. There is no need for any special inoculations, but the sun can be very strong, so you should take ample sun protection, and it's probably wise to take insect repellent and sting relief products.

ENTRY FORMALITIES

Documentation

Passports are needed by UK visitors and all others except EU citizens who can produce a national identity card. Visits of up to three months do not require a visa if you are a national of the USA, Canada, Australia or New Zealand. Other travellers should consult the French embassy, consulate or Tourist Information office in their own country regarding visa requirements. You can also check France's Ministry of Foreign Affairs website, which provides information for all nationalities (ⓦ www.diplomatie.gouv.fr).

Customs

Residents of the UK, Ireland and other EU countries may bring into France personal possessions and goods for personal use, including a reasonable amount of tobacco and alcohol, provided they have been bought in the EU. There are few formalities at the points of entry into France. Residents of non-EU countries, and EU residents arriving from a non-EU country, may bring in up to 400 cigarettes and 50 cigars or 50 g (2 oz) of tobacco, 2 litres (3 bottles) of wine and 1 litre (approx. 2 pints) of spirits and liqueurs.

MONEY

The euro (€) is the official currency in France. €1 is equal to 100 cents. The euro comes in notes of €5, €10, €20, €50, €100, €200 and €500. Coins are in denominations of €1 and €2, and 1, 2, 5, 10, 20 and 50 cents.

ATM machines can be found at Nice airport and larger railway stations, and are widely available around the Côte d'Azur. They accept most British and international debit and credit cards. They are the quickest and most convenient way (and often the cheapest) to obtain cash. Instructions are usually available in English and other major European languages.

Credit cards are almost universally accepted, except sometimes at smaller shops, cafés and markets. You will have to know your pin numbers, as the chip-and-pin system is normally used in France. Note that some shops and other establishments have a lower limit, below which they won't accept cards. Some places won't accept American Express or Diners' cards.

You will also have no difficulty finding banks (including branches of some British banks in Cannes, Nice and Monaco, for instance) and bureaux de change. But be aware that the latter often offer very poor rates of exchange.

CLIMATE

With 300 annual days of sunshine, the Côte d'Azur attracts visitors throughout the year. Winters are mild with temperatures averaging 12°C (53°F) during the day. Evenings can, however, be cold. Spring and autumn days are sometimes hot, but more usually warm, with chilly evenings (partly because of the mistral wind) and some heavy rainfall. Summers can get hot, with temperatures sometimes exceeding 30°C (86°F), and you might experience an occasional thunderstorm.

Because of the weather, summers can be very crowded; accommodation can be difficult to find unless you book well in advance, and hotel (and often bar and restaurant) prices are much higher. Hotels become packed during major events, and some hotels and restaurants close in winter, so always check.

BAGGAGE ALLOWANCE

At the time of writing, baggage allowances and restrictions have been significantly altered in the light of terrorist threats. Although this mainly applies to hand luggage, some restrictions also apply to hold luggage. At the same time, several airlines, particularly low-cost carriers, are changing guidelines or introducing charges for checked-in baggage. You are advised to check with your carrier shortly before you fly. The airline websites all have baggage allowance information and a list of prohibited items.

◐ *The buses are frequent and easy to use*

During your stay

AIRPORTS

The only airport conveniently serving the area is Nice-Côte d'Azur. Although it is the second most important in France in terms of passenger volume, it is small in terms of major international hubs, and is fairly quick to get through. You will be able to find shops, banks, bureaux de change, bars and ATMs on arrival. The airport is just 7 km (4 miles) from the centre of Nice, and the city is easy to get to. You can go by bus (from outside Terminal 1) to the centre of town (Bus 98 & 99) or to Nice-Ville station (Bus 23). It takes around 30 minutes and the fares are modest. Taxis are easily available but very expensive. All the major car hire companies are represented at the airport. The pick-up point is outside Terminal 2, which you can reach with a free shuttle bus.
If your destination is Monaco, you also have the option of travelling by helicopter with Héli Air Monaco. It isn't cheap, but it's a spectacular ride, and it can sometimes cost less than taking a taxi if there are only two of you (● Office at airport ⓦ www.heliairmonaco.com).
Nice-Côte d'Azur Airport ❶ Flight information 0820 42 33 33
ⓦ www.nice.aeroport.fr

COMMUNICATIONS
Phones

Card-operated public phone booths are everywhere, and you can make international calls from them. You can buy phone cards (*télécartes*) at *tabacs* (newsagent/tobacconists sporting a red diamond sign outside), post offices and some cafés and railway stations. Some public phones also accept credit cards. Insert the card after lifting the receiver. You can also make follow-on calls.

There is good mobile phone coverage, though you will have to switch to a local network such as SFR. Check with your service provider before you leave to find out which will be the cheapest for you.

TELEPHONING FRANCE

To call the Côte d'Azur from outside France, dial the international prefix (oo in most countries) followed by France's country code (33), then the area code minus the initial o (4), and the eight-digit local number.

To call the Côte d'Azur from anywhere in France, dial the full area code (04), followed by the eight-digit local number.

❶ 06 is the prefix for mobile numbers in France.

TELEPHONING MONACO

To call Monaco from anywhere else in the world (including France), the international access code (oo) must be followed by 377, then the local number. The Monaco numbers given in this book are all local.

TELEPHONING ABROAD

To call overseas from France or Monaco, dial oo for an international connection, followed by your country code (UK 44, Republic of Ireland 353, USA and Canada 1, Australia 61, New Zealand 64, South Africa 27) and then the area code (leaving out the first o if there is one) and the local number.

❶ When calling France from Monaco, remember that you have to dial oo and the country code 33, before dialling the area code (without the initial o) and the local number.

Local directory enquiries 12
International operator oo 33 12 + country code

Post

Post offices can be found throughout the area, in even the smallest towns. They open 09.00–19.00 on weekdays (some closing 12.00–14.00), and close on Saturday afternoons and Sundays. Small local offices may

close earlier during the week. You can buy stamps there or in *tabacs*.
The postal service is efficient, and postcards to the UK and Ireland will
normally arrive in 2–3 days, taking a little longer to non-European

🔺 *An internet café with a postbox outside*

destinations. Current rates for sending postcards are €0.50 to Europe, and €0.90 to North America, Australia and New Zealand.

❶ Only Monaco stamps can be used on mail posted in the principality, and they can't be used on mail posted in France.

Internet

Internet access is widespread on the Côte d'Azur, with internet cafés easily found in larger towns and major resorts, although not necessarily in small villages. Check for addresses with your hotel or Tourist Information. All but the simplest hotels provide internet connections.

CUSTOMS

There are no special local customs to be aware of, but it's a generally well-heeled area, and holiday-makers are expected to behave with decorum, particularly in Monaco. Drunkenness and noisy, rude or rowdy behaviour are frowned upon. And children are expected to be well behaved, particularly in restaurants.

DRESS CODES

Most people wear casual clothes during the day and smart-casual during the evening, although you will also see many smartly dressed locals and visitors. Bathing costumes are fine for beach and pool-side restaurants, but they are discouraged in shops, attractions and public areas of hotels. Most people dress smartly at the main casinos (jacket and tie are required in Monte-Carlo Casino) and in leading restaurants.

ELECTRICITY

France runs on 220 V and uses two-pin plugs. British appliances will need a simple adaptor, best obtained in most UK electrical shops or at the Eurostar station or airport. You should also be able to find shops at your destination selling adaptors, but you might have difficulty finding them in smaller towns. US and other equipment designed for 110 V will need a transformer as well.

EMERGENCIES

NATIONAL FREE EMERGENCY PHONE NUMBERS
All emergency services 112 (this number must be used when calling from a mobile phone)
Medical/ambulance (SAMU) 15
Police (Gendarmerie) 17
Fire (Sapeurs-Pompiers) 18

Hospitals & medical centres
General practitioners can be found in all but the smallest places, as can dentists. It's best to ask your hotel or Tourist Information for the nearest English-speaking ones. The larger towns all have hospitals, and will have some doctors who speak English.

Antibes Hospital Centre Hospitalier d'Antibes ⓐ 7 route Nationale, 06600 Antibes ⓣ 04 92 91 77 77

Cannes Hospital Centre Hospitalier de Cannes ⓐ 15 avenue Broussailles, 06400 Cannes ⓣ Emergencies 04 93 69 71 50; switchboard 04 93 69 70 00

Grasse Hospital Centre Hospitalier de Grasse ⓐ Chemin de Clavery, 06135 Grasse ⓣ 04 93 09 55 55

Monaco Hospital Centre Hospitalier Princesse Grace ⓐ Avenue Pasteur ⓣ 97 98 99 00

Nice Hospital Hôpital St-Roch ⓐ 5 rue Pierre Devoluy ⓣ 04 92 03 33 75

Riviera Medical Services An on-call service with English-speaking doctors (not necessarily for emergencies). ⓣ 04 93 26 12 70

SOS Dentaire Emergency dental care at night and on Sundays and public holidays. ⓣ 04 93 76 53 53

Police
The major police stations (in Nice, for instance) usually have interpreters available.

Antibes Police Municipale ⓐ 39 boulevard Président Wilson ⓣ 04 92 93 05 24

Cannes Commissariat de Police ⊜ 1 avenue Grasse ☎ 04 93 06 22 22
Monaco Sûreté Publique (lost property) ⊜ 3 rue Louis Notari
☎ 93 15 30 18
Police Municipale ⊜ Place Marie ☎ 93 15 28 26
Nice Commissariat Central de Police ⊜ 1 avenue Maréchal Foch
☎ 04 92 17 22 22
Police Municipale (lost property) ⊜ 1 rue de la Terrasse ☎ 04 97 13 44 00

Consulates & embassies
Australian Embassy ⊜ 4 rue Jean Rey, Paris ☎ 01 40 59 33 00
Canadian Consulate ⊜ 10 rue Lamartine, Nice ☎ 04 93 92 93 22
New Zealand Embassy ⊜ 7 rue Léonard da Vinci, Paris ☎ 01 45 01 43 43
Republic of Ireland Consulate ⊜ 152 boulevard J-F Kennedy, Cap d'Antibes
South African Honorary Consul General ⊜ 30 boulevard Princesse
Charlotte, Monaco ☎ 93 25 24 26
UK Consulate General ⊜ 24 avenue du Prado, Marseille ☎ 04 91 15 72 10
UK Honorary Consul ⊜ 33 boulevard Princesse Charlotte, Monaco
☎ 93 50 99 54
USA Consulate ⊜ 7 avenue Gustave V, 3rd Floor, Nice ☎ 04 93 88 89 55

EMERGENCY PHRASES

Help!	Au secours!	*Oh secoor!*
Help me!	Aidez-moi!	*Ayday mwa!*
Call the police	Appelez la police	*Up-i-lay la poleece*
Stop!	Stop!	*Stop!*
Stop thief!	Au voleur!	*Oh volerr!*
Call a doctor	Appelez un médecin	*Up-i-lay a med-e-san*
Fire!	Au feu!	*Oh-fur (without pronouncing the 'r')*
Leave me alone!	Laissez-moi tranquille!	*Laysay mwa trawn-keel*

GETTING AROUND

Driving

You can drive in France with a valid licence (held for at least a year) from an EU country or one from the USA or Canada. Remember to also bring your insurance and other relevant documents.

French traffic drives on the right, and at junctions without stop signs you must give way to traffic coming from the right. You and your passengers must always wear a seat belt. Children below the age of 10 must sit in the back. Check for other regulations with your motoring organisation.

You will have to have cash or a credit card on you to pay for toll roads. Motorways have rest areas with restaurants, shops and petrol stations at regular intervals. They are indicated by the word 'aire' followed by the name of the location.

Many roads on the Côte d'Azur, particularly the main coastal roads, can become very congested in the summer, and in rush hour in cities like Nice. Most places also have one-way systems, which can sometimes be complex.

Parking can often be a problem, particularly in summer, but you can usually find pay and display areas in larger towns, as well as car parks. Hill towns and smaller resorts usually have car parks at their entrance, but they can get crowded, so it's best to go early or late. Many larger hotels and restaurants have their own car parks.

Car hire

There are plenty of car hire places, particularly at the airport, large railway stations and in cities such as Nice and Cannes, but car hire is expensive in France. It often pays to book a car with your flight or train, or to organise car hire before you leave home. To be allowed to hire a car, you have to be over 25 and have had a licence for a year, but people aged 21–25 can sometimes hire a car if they pay a supplement. Remember to take your licence and passport to the hire office. Some hotels will organise car hire for you, and arrange for the car to be delivered to the hotel.

Public transport

Bus services are pretty good along the coast and in major towns. Larger towns normally have a bus station (*gare routière*), often near the railway station. You can get route maps and timetables at your local Tourist Information office.

The main local bus service, the Ligne d'Azur, which has routes within Nice and to most of the destinations mentioned in this book, has flat fares, and you can also buy one-day and seven-day passes or multi-journey tickets. Buy your tickets from the driver. You can also buy passes and multi-journey tickets from *tabacs*. You must validate your pass every time you board by sticking it into the small machine at the front of the bus. You dismount from the door in the middle of the bus. The Ligne d'Azur has a comprehensive and helpful website from which you can

⏷ *The coastal train service is fairly fast and frequent*

download maps and timetables. If you intend to travel by bus, it's well worth looking at before you leave home.
Ⓦ www.lignedazur.com

The local inter-city bus service is run by TAM (Transport Alpes-Maritimes). You can check timetables and routes on their website.
Ⓦ www.cg06.fr/transport/transports-tam.html

The coastal train service is very good, and the trains are pretty fast and frequent. It is a very good way to explore the coast. Fares are moderate. You can buy tickets at the machines found at the railway stations, which have instructions in English. Check the timetables (and their many notes) carefully if travelling out of season.

Taxis

You will rarely need to take taxis to get around smaller destinations, as you can usually walk, but you may need to catch a taxi in places such as Nice and Cannes. They are very expensive, particularly if you decide to take taxis between towns or to the airport. Taxis have meters, although drivers often don't turn them on, and you will be charged extra for luggage. They are even more expensive at night, so make sure you have plenty of cash on you. Taxis can be found at ranks (particularly at rail and bus stations), or your hotel or restaurant will be able to call you one. Otherwise you can call Central Taxi Riviera (☏ 04 93 13 78 78).

HEALTH, SAFETY & CRIME

It is safe to drink tap water, as most people do, although some prefer to drink mineral water. There are no major precautions you need to take when eating local food, but since seafood is likely to be on most menus, you might be unlucky, and you would be sensible to bring suitable tablets, such as Imodium, to settle your stomach. Buying cooked food from street stalls might also cause problems, but on the whole, you need worry no more than at home.

Medical care in France is of a very high standard but expensive unless you have suitable travel insurance. Most minor ailments can be dealt with at pharmacies, of which there are many, all indicated by green cross signs. They have staff who are qualified to offer medical advice and dispense a wide range of medicines.

The Côte d'Azur is generally safe, but you should be careful in cities such as Nice and Cannes late at night. Otherwise, as in many holiday destinations, you should guard against bag snatchers (a particular problem in Nice) and pickpockets by taking sensible precautions such as keeping your bag or camera close to you and making sure that you don't keep valuables in your back pocket, or carry more money than you need. Also be careful about your bag and camera when sitting at street tables outside restaurants and cafés, and in crowded places such as railway stations and street markets. Car crime can also be a problem, so never leave anything valuable visible in your car. You will also encounter beggars, whom you should avoid, and the odd hustler and con artist. It's safest to avoid conversation and simply walk on.

Most of the main tourist destinations have police patrols. In general, the police try to be helpful, but might not speak English. There are three main types of police. The Police Municipale are the ones you are most likely to see in towns; they oversee traffic and deal with petty crime and lost property. The Police Nationale deal with more serious matters in larger towns. In country districts and on motorways, the Gendarmerie Nationale, a military force, is the main law enforcement body. If you are robbed, you should make a statement at your nearest police station to make an insurance claim.

MEDIA

A number of British newspapers, such as the *Daily Mail*, are now also printed in France and available on the day at many newsagents. The same applies to the *International Herald Tribune*. There are also local English-language newspapers such as the *Riviera Reporter* and the *Riviera Times*. In cities such as Nice, Monte-Carlo and Cannes, you can also get local listings magazines in English, such as the quarterly *Anglo Riviera Guide* which is distributed to hotels and Tourist Information offices.

Many hotels have satellite TV with channels such as BBC World, Sky News and CNN. There is also Riviera Radio, an English-speaking station on 106.3/106.5 FM.

OPENING HOURS

Shops are generally open 09.00–12.00 & 14.00–19.00 Mon–Sat, but shops in tourist areas are often open all day and on Sundays, and have later closing times. Bakeries usually open earlier. Some shops close on Mondays.

● *Pharmacies are easy to spot*

Markets usually open at 08.00 or 09.00 and start packing up around 12.30. It's best to go early to avoid the crowds.

Public offices are usually open 08.30–12.00 & 14.00–18.00 Mon–Fri.

Banks open 08.30–12.00 & 13.30–17.00 Mon–Fri, though times may vary slightly; some banks open all day, for instance. They are always closed on public holidays.

The opening times of museums and attractions vary. But they are normally open 10.00–18.00 or 19.00 in summer. However, some (usually smaller museums) close for lunch, and most have shorter hours outside the high season. Some also close on public holidays and on either Monday or Tuesday. Entrance to bigger museums sometimes ends 30 minutes before closing.

TIME DIFFERENCES

French clocks follow Central European Time (CET). During Daylight Saving Time (end Mar–end Oct), the clocks are put ahead 1 hour. In the French summer, at noon, times elsewhere are as follows:

Australia Eastern Standard Time 20.00, Central Standard Time 19.30, Western Standard Time 18.00

New Zealand 22.00

South Africa 12.00

UK and Republic of Ireland 11.00

USA and Canada Newfoundland Time 07.30, Atlantic Canada Time 07.00, Eastern Time 06.00, Central Time 05.00, Mountain Time 04.00, Pacific Time 03.00, Alaska 02.00

TIPPING

There is no need to tip in restaurants, bars and cafés, as service is included. But most people leave some small change, or more if they have had exceptional service. Taxi drivers and people who provide services such as hairdressing should be tipped 10–15 per cent. If you are in a smart hotel where your bags are carried to your room, you might tip with a one- or two-euro coin.

TOILETS

You should have no difficulty finding a toilet on the Côte d'Azur. Public buildings, such as museums, usually have clean and modern toilets in the publicly accessible areas near the entrance. The fastest and easiest solution is usually to step into a bar or café and have a quick drink there. Note that some smaller establishments still have the old French hole-in-the-ground loos, which many people find off-putting. A much more salubrious alternative is to pop into one of the better hotels for a drink; here you will find marbled luxury. There are also public toilets (often modern, coin-operated cubicles) at the airport and train stations, and in many other public toilets you may have to pay a small fee (normally €0.50).

TRAVELLERS WITH DISABILITIES

A number of museums, restaurants and hotels have access facilities usable by visitors with mobility problems, and the bigger towns also have wheelchair-accessible road crossings. But it must be said that hill villages, and the older parts of some towns, with their cobbled streets, ancient buildings, pedestrianised areas, large number of tourists and limited flow for motor vehicles, aren't the ideal destinations for visitors with mobility issues. And although you might be able to get a wheelchair on to local buses and trains, taxis aren't adapted. Useful organisations for advice and information include:

Association des Paralysés de France Délégation Départemental des Alpes-Maritimes ⓐ 21 boulevard Mantéga-Righi, Nice ⓣ 04 92 15 78 70

RADAR The principal UK forum and pressure group for people with disabilities. ⓐ 12 City Forum, 250 City Road, London EC1V 8AF ⓣ (020) 7250 3222 ⓦ www.radar.org.uk

SATH (Society for Accessible Travel & Hospitality) Advises US-based travellers with disabilities. ⓐ 347 Fifth Ave, Suite 610, New York, NY 10016 ⓣ (212) 447 7284 ⓦ www.sath.org

ACKNOWLEDGEMENTS

The publishers would like to thank the following individuals and organisations for providing their copyright photographs for this book: Fotolia/Philippe Devanne page 74; all the rest, Anwer Bati.

Copy editor: Anne McGregor
Proofreader: Ian Faulkner

Send your thoughts to
books@thomascook.com

- Found a beach bar, peaceful stretch of sand or must-see sight that we don't feature?

- Like to tip us off about any information that needs a little updating?

- Want to tell us what you love about this handy, little guidebook and more importantly how we can make it even handier?

Then here's your chance to tell all! Send us ideas, discoveries and recommendations today and then look out for your valuable input in the next edition of this title. And, as an extra 'thank you' from Thomas Cook Publishing, you'll be automatically entered into our exciting prize draw.

Send an email to the above address or write to:
HotSpots Project Editor, Thomas Cook Publishing, PO Box 227, Unit 18, Coningsby Road, Peterborough PE3 8SB, UK